COLUMNISTS:

While We're Still Around

By Garret Mathews

Cover photos by MaryAnne Mathews
Illustrations by Mark Coomer

ISBN 978-1-312-19072-6

http://www.columnists-stillaround.com

Table of Contents

Introduction

The job I so loved for so long is on life-support. This gathering of columns is my way of breathing life into the profession for at least as long as it takes readers to turn the pages.

Thousands of reporters and editors have lost their jobs in recent years as newspapers have downsized until some editions don't weigh much more than a doily. The number of full-time local columnists on metro and features staffs has tumbled to a mere few.

Some of us accepted buyouts. Some were let go. Some, like me, were reassigned to other beats, didn't much care for it and counted down the days until we were old enough for Social Security.

Soon, I fear, column-writing for newspapers will exist only in yellowed clippings from yesteryear.

At the risk of sounding too self-important, I think the silencing of these voices is a slash in the fabric of Americana.

In 2009, two years after I lost my five-days-a-week space in the Evansville, Ind., Courier & Press, I put together a book of 75 or so columns from my time in the Midwest.

"Favorites" is the title. It can be accessed for free at www.newspaperwriter.com.

From the introduction:

"Sue me, but I'm not interested in writing about who's going to win the mayor's race, or why didn't the City Council adopt the Westside sewage plan, or should more riverboat money be used to improve the city's infrastructure.

"I'd rather talk with a demolition derby driver, or an old-timer who hand-loaded 49 tons of coal in a single shift, or the fellow of modest means who gave $2,000 back to the government to help pay down the national debt because he believed it was the patriotic thing to do.

"I liked to write goof pieces about throwing my 16-pound shot put in the back yard, and finding out how far I can walk carrying a 25-pound pack, and organizing an Over-40 baseball team that played a series of games against Pony League all-stars. Because it was my idea, I got to pitch. And I hit .350.

"I've always believed that the quirky and the down-and-out are more interesting than persons who hang out in office buildings. Those eyeballing my portion of the page could expect to read about an exotic dancer who wanted to be a herpetologist, or the 91-year-old lady who got caught (again) for bootlegging whisky, or the pauper who died and the only people who showed up for the burial (besides me) were the two guys from the funeral home.

"Why am I doing this book? Because I don't want to be forgotten. When my grandchildren come along, I want them to know what their Pop-Pop did for a living. This is my way of climbing to the highest building, opening the window and hollering out, "Once upon a time, I did this thing for a living and I'm very proud of it."

If nothing else, I was relentless. Counting the ones I wrote for the Bluefield, W. Va., Daily Telegraph between 1972 and 1987, I penned more than 6,500 columns until my old-enough day came in 2011 and I retired.

Which means I have time on my hands.

Which leads to this collection.

For "Favorites," I preserved some of my work for posterity.

For "While We're Still Around," I'm providing a haven for columns of other men and women of similar mind who entertain (or entertained) countless readers with their prose.

I don't want them to be forgotten. If these folks don't have access to a skyscraper and an open window, they can use mine.

It's my tribute to our wonderful profession.

After the last newspaper is printed, waves of nostalgia will wash over the land. Once-upon-a-time columnists will become point-persons for the queries of the curious.

What was it like, they'll wonder, back when the dawning of a new day meant the plopping of millions of newspapers on millions of porches? Was it true, they'll want to know, that the race was on after the plop, and the household member the most willing to open the front door the least dressed was the one to claim the prize? And was it true that at least 75 percent of the DNA of living room lamp switches was newsprint?

When called, I'll testify to the great joy on my first night at the Daily Telegraph when I discovered the only technology required was the ability to put a sheet of paper into the manual typewriter. I'll further spout that I do not do Facebook, do not tweet and do not own a phone that's any smarter than I am. When I see "app," I think somebody misspelled the abbreviation for Associated Press.

I'll recall a time when the words "relevant" and "newspapers" were always found in the same sentence.

Monday Night Football games ended after the midnight deadline at the West Virginia newspaper. The publisher insisted the front sports page be replated to report the final score, and never mind if we had to stay late and miss the first round of beer. The reasoning was sound. There were no local cut-ins on the "Today Show," and if news crawls at the bottom of the screen had been invented by the early 1970s, they certainly hadn't arrived in that corner of the Mountain State. If the late game wasn't in the newspaper, it was a good bet the results wouldn't be common knowledge until the Tuesday evening TV newscast.

Our Depression-era press turned pretty much every half-tone into a black glob, and the ruled eight-column format made it impossible to create page layouts that were the least bit attractive. It didn't matter. The population of the three largest towns in the circulation area was around 27,000. We sold that many daily papers and more. A penetration rate to die for.

I'll lament the sad fact that many newspapers have become little more than final resting places for press releases. Overworked editors see them by the hundreds when they open their in-boxes. In large part, the next day's edition is filled with those items selected to be rewritten by the few wages-frozen reporters still on the payroll.

I'll recall a brighter era when newsrooms had enough hands on deck for a thorough report not only of developments in the city where the product was printed, but in the hinterlands. Folks living two counties over and 100 miles away still considered the paper their own.

This golden age meant there was room for columnists. Lots of them, and not just on the big dailies. In Evansville, the tradition of having a metro columnist dates back to the 1950s.

This collection celebrates those good times.

Men and women like me made you laugh, stirred your emotions and introduced you to characters you otherwise would never have known.

I believe every card-carrying adult (re: civilian) has 15 or 20 columns in them. The eccentric relative. The high school chum who hit it rich. Or poor. The funny story the guy in the next cubicle tells about closing his first deal.

I believe reporters and editors have 45 or 50 tucked aside -- thanks to professional writing chops and professional observational skills – before running out of gas.

That's the difference.

Columnists refuel.

So who's in the book?

Sentimentality plays a part. Again, sue me. As a kid growing up in Abingdon, Va., I loved the whimsical pieces of Ben Beagle in the Roanoke Times. I couldn't do this project and leave him out.

Johnny Blankenship was in the newsroom on my first night. He's in. So is Louise Leslie, who for decades penned a column for the weekly in nearby Tazewell, Va. As a young deskman in Bluefield, I looked forward to opening packets from the Newspaper Enterprise Association and reading the latest from Tom Tiede. He roamed the country digging up feature stories and I envied him greatly.

I'm familiar with some folks in these pages from my occasional membership in the National Society of Newspaper Columnists. I trolled the Internet to find other writers whose work I like.

In my pitch letter, I asked the men and women to submit columns that show their personalities. I told them I wasn't interested in red-state, blue-state stuff or their stand on abortion.

Ageism is in play here. I sought out folks who have been at it a long time. The longer their memories, the better.

My thrust is print journalism because that's what I know best, but there are a few bloggers in here so I won't be accused of being completely old-fashioned.

So, columnists, and civilians who follow our ramblings, let's raise our shot glasses and share a toast.

While we're still around.

Garret Mathews
garretmath@gmail.com
May 20, 2014

Mark Coomer, my colleague for many years at the Evansville Courier & Press, drew the illustrations that accompany some of the columns.

My wife, MaryAnne, and my daughter-in-law, Rachael Mathews, helped with editing.

This column by Garret Mathews appeared on January 20, 2002, in the Evansville Courier & Press.

Ragu Sauce And The Start
Of A Newspaper Career

Thirty years ago this week, I packed my worldly possessions into a Ford Pinto and took off down the road for my first newspaper job at the Bluefield, W. Va., Daily Telegraph. Because I wasn't very worldly, I only needed half the trunk.

I arranged to live in a boarding house. The eighty-something owner said we would get along just fine.

There were just a few rules.

I would pay the week's $10 rent on Saturday no earlier than 9 a.m. before she was properly dressed. And no later than 10 a.m. when she left on foot for the bank.

I could not commit anything that could even remotely be construed as noise.

I could not use the hall telephone longer than 60 seconds. An egg timer was beside the receiver as a reminder.

I could only use one towel a day.

"This is a place of residence, not a laundry," she liked to say.

And I couldn't bring women up to my room.

"Morals of this country are going to the devil," she said, fanning herself with a church bulletin. "If I can help just one boy from going bad…"

I wanted to go bad in the worst way, but living on the Telegraph's $90 a week was akin to giving me a Good Conduct Medal.

I looked around the room. Bed, desk, mirror, cabinet, Book of Psalms, closet, decorative urn of Noah leading the animals into the ark and two washcloths carefully folded to look like praying hands.

The Vienna sausages I had for lunch were working on me. I went in the bathroom, sat on the commode and contemplated my future.

Suddenly, the woman burst in.

I tried to cover up, but my shirt was too short.

"Where you from anyway?"

Stammering and embarrassed, I told her.

"Do you know the Pullams? Bob and Jane. They're from down that way."

Desperately, I began making grunting and straining noises, hoping to get her to leave.

"Real nice people. Never miss a worship service."

She looked at her watch.

"Got to make supper. Don't forget to wash your hands."

I had just enough time to take a bath before going to work. The knobs looked like they had been installed during the Roaring Twenties, so I didn't expect much. But to my surprise, hot and cold surged out of the appropriate taps.

I lathered up and hoped I hadn't forgotten to pack my Gregg Typing Manual. If I couldn't impress my co-workers with my smarts, I could at least get them to appreciate my keystrokes.

I looked down at my feet. They were bright red.

There was no pain, so it couldn't be blood. I leaned over and saw Ragu Sauce coming up from the drain. Lots of it.

I quickly used up my towel allotment. The rest of the dry-off was with an undershirt.

"You've got to do something about the bathtub," I said, storming into the kitchen. "My legs look like dinner."

"Oh, it's those darn pipes again."

She explained that the plumbing in the kitchen sink is connected to the plumbing in the bathtub. When stuff goes down the one, stuff comes up the other.

"I'll pray on it, and if that doesn't work, I'll call the handyman down the street."

That night, I laid out the stock market page, proofed the obits and wrote headlines on a stack of briefs from the Old Guard electing officers to the next meeting of the Bluewell Public Service District.

Occasionally, my pants legs rode up. My co-workers laughed and called me "Red Man."

I was on my way.

August 27, 2002

Aces, Studs And Slicks
From Those Days Of Yore

When I recall my early years in the newspaper business at the Bluefield, W. Va., Daily Telegraph, I think of pounding out stories on an ancient Royal typewriter that could have been used as a barbell at a World War II boot camp.

And mailroom guys growing marijuana in the dirt between the cracks of the wood floor on the third floor.

C.W., their boss, was cool with it and even helped with the harvest.

"Makes 'em work better," he told me.

And never completely trusting the contents of the pizza on my desk because pieces of the Depression-era ceiling were always falling down. One night, a staffer thought he was biting into an anchovy and ended up needing dental work.

I worked with a narc, a woman who went to jail for Social Security fraud, a guy who went to jail for assault, assorted alcoholics, assorted drug users and a deskman who tried to burn the newspaper building down.

The attempted mass homicide didn't amount to much. The gothic structure had lived through 80 years of storms, pigeons, angry readers and poor reporters. It could survive a quart of lighter fluid and a boat-load of matches.

But what I remember most are the nicknames that were given out like lollipops at the bank.

The big three were "slick," "ace" and "stud."

As in:

"Gimme six grafs on that bus wreck, slick, so we can make deadline and go drink beer at the King Tut Drive-In before Stu tries to set the place on fire again."

And:

"Hang up on your girlfriend, stud. Need that headline on the Sewage Board meeting some time today. We ain't a monthly."

And:

"Better not be going up to the mailroom, ace. The cops are up there and they ain't friendlies."

And:

"I know there's no chair, slick. Company policy. There's three for every five employees. Either come in early or learn to squat."

And:

"Wouldn't park out front if I was you, ace. Get a little wind and bricks start flying off the roof. Usually land where your hood ornament is."

Sadly, you don't hear those wonderful nouns around the newspaper office any more.

We have this ridiculous, politically correct notion that folks should be called by their real names.

Can't call somebody "slick" because it means "pile of bile" to natives of Qatar.

Can't call somebody "ace" because it reminds the news editor he isn't one.

Newsrooms are alleged to be too sophisticated to dabble in such verbiage these days. We have carpet now. And coffee makers. And ceilings that stand their ground.

I take this opportunity to break from the mold.

MEMO:

To: Those who address me in the future

From: The columnist in cubicle 12

Let it be known that henceforth I will no longer answer to Garret. Or GM. Or "Whatsit." Or "Hey, you."

I want my appellation to touch on the rich history of the newspaper business.

I also want it to reflect my strength, power, well-being and, yes, virility.

My greeting of choice is "stud."

As in:

"Hey, stud, the company car is stuck in a ditch. Wanna lift it out for us?"

And:

"Hey, stud, our new hire was parking his car and got hit with a brick. Can we borrow some of your scar tissue?"

And:

"Hey, stud, there's a gas leak at the Tut. Can you suck up the fumes until the HAZ-MAT crews get here? And hurry. There are three slicks and two aces trapped in the bar."

Mark Patinkin writes for the Providence, R.I., Journal. He has won three New England Emmy Awards for television commentaries. This column appeared June 9, 2013.

Four Years As College Athlete Flew By Too Fast

As he stood in the pre-game huddle, 39 teammates around him, helmets touching, he knew this could be it, the last game, not just the end of the season but of his ride as a college athlete.

Or it could be the moment he'd hoped for since freshman year. They'd made it to the league championship. A win would take the Babson College lacrosse team to the national playoffs for the first time since 1979.

The sun was strong and he began to sweat under his pads. It got him thinking back to the freezing games of February, when show was piled high on the side of the field. And then the rainy games of March. That's spring sports in New England, he thought; too cold, too wet, too hot.

Yet that's partly why he became a college athlete: to test himself. To see if he could measure up when it's hard. His teammates felt the same, and together, they'd done it. They'd shared 6 a.m. lifts and silent bus rides after painful defeats by some of the best teams in the country, like Tufts. They'd shared the highs, too, and all of it's what made them a family.

He looked around the huddle, remembering that first season when he felt college lacrosse would last forever. He'd put up 55 points that year, and the next, an almost record-breaking 67. It had been some ride. But now, four years later, here he was.

How did it go by so fast?

He told himself they had to win this game – buy themselves a ticket to the NCAA Division III bracket. At least once, he wanted to go to that dance. But there was another reason, too. He wasn't ready for it to stop. This is who he was. A college athlete. Whether on the field, in the messy dorm lacrosse suite, or simply as an identity, it's where he felt at home in this world.

He could not imagine it coming to an end. And so abruptly. That's how it is after your last game as a senior. You ride the bus home, turn in your equipment and a lifetime playing a competitive sport is over.

He still had the same number, 13, that he'd worn since high school at Providence Country Day. That was important to him, in the way ritual is important to all athletes. It's why no one had shaved since they made the Pilgrim League playoffs – even the coach hadn't because whatever they did, they did as a team.

And now the huddle broke and as one of the captains, he jogged to the pre-game talk with the refs, then took up position as lefty attack. They were playing away, at Springfield College, their arch-rival. He watched as the midis squared off for opening faceoff.

It was his 70th college game, but other kinds of statistics were just as important. For every hour of play, there had been at least 20 hours of practice, maybe more. There were the four spring breaks missed because athletes in season stay on campus. There were countless strategy meetings and hundreds of nights on pre-game lockdown while your friends partied. The media attention is on Division I teams, but he knew that for the 150,000 or so college athletes who play Division III in America, the experience is almost as consuming.

And then the game started, and in a huge moment, Babson notched the first goal. God, he loved those moments, the way teammates swarm the shooter and the whole roster explodes on the sidelines. He doubted there are as many venues when colleagues so joyfully celebrate each other's success.

He remembered one of the best such moments only a week before, when he was at this same field for his final regular season game, on the brink of a milestone. And he did it, putting in two goals to break Babson's 32-year record for career points with a total of 232. His team went wild for him, but he felt it was theirs, too, because goals in lacrosse belong as much to the defenseman who forced the turnover a minute before as to you.

He felt the same high now as Babson drew first blood. But his mood dropped minutes later when Springfield came back with a goal of its own. And then another. As the periods went by, the gap widened. A week before, Babson was up 9-3 at the half against this same team. Now, they were down 7-2.

And he felt it happening – that indefinable something that throws a team off its game. Babson couldn't get it back, and the clock would not slow down. Suddenly, only one minute was left and it was 14-3. He got the last pass and as the buzzer sounded, made a no-chance shot as his way of saying goodbye.

And then it was over.

The game. The season. His college career.

They had not done it.

As Springfield raced into a victory pile, he stood quietly with his teammates, greasepaint dripping down their faces, looking like warriors, but in truth, he knew there are few times when young men like this are more fragile.

He kept his helmet on during the handshake because he didn't want anyone to see. He kept it on as he headed off the field.

Through the gate.

Where the Babson fans had gathered quietly.

Myself among them.

"Alex," I said, and hugged him around his jersey and pads. He hugged me back.

It had been a long time since my son cried this hard.

I told him I loved him. Choking out the words, he said the same to me.

As his shoulders shook, I told him one more thing: "Son, it was the ride of my life, too."

He was only able to nod.

And then I watched as Number 13, head down, walked to the post-game lockers for the last time.

June 19, 2010

Divorce Day: One Life Ends And Another Begins

Four months later, I still remember the cold. The temperature was in the teens. It had been that way for

weeks, and the ice patches on the streets in downtown
Providence were hard as a rock. I left behind a coat,
thinking it wouldn't be easy to check it at Family Court.
As I walked from the parking lot at 9 a.m., I put my
hands in my suit jacket pockets and hunched into myself.
They say the weather at times mirrors the spirit. Indeed.

Some things are too hard to write about when you are
close to them. It is only now that I can bring myself to
revisit that February day.

There was a long line out the courthouse door. As I
waited, I looked across the river to the historic homes on
the East Side. To the south, they were moving the
highways to create a changed city – the old still there, as
it would always be, and yet on the brink of new
beginnings.

They handle divorces on the fifth floor. I had been
there before as a journalist, writing about how, after
years of shared lives, it comes down to a division of
assets – who gets the dishes, who the children. No one
expects to find themselves on this floor, but if the
statistics are correct, for half of married people, it is a
matter of time.

The hallway was crowded and many folks looked
strained. There are few parts of life with deeper emotion.
The process is full of heartache. If only he'd done
this…or she that. But beneath it all, the explanation is
usually simple. People change. That's all.

I found my lawyer, and my wife found hers, and soon,
the four of us were sitting in a small meeting space
outside our courtroom. It was like the end of any
business negotiation. Paperwork was passed back and

forth, the agreements signed, and then I was on the witness stand.

Matter called, ready nominal, and it began.

My lawyer stood. My role would be perfunctory. When a divorce is uncontested, the final hearing is simply about the facts.

"You were married in May 10, 1986, in Massachusetts. Is that correct?"

"Yes," I said, and said no more. But I thought back to that day. We had wanted to be married outdoors, and chose a country inn, under a tree in spring bloom. I liked the symbol of that. I was 33 and she 29. I had been slow to the altar, but one day, a man finds his partner, and he's ready. Divorce often makes people look back on their choice as a mistake, but that's seldom true. Over the years, most people live more than one life. At the time, it was the perfect union.

"Have you been continuously domiciled in and a resident of the State of Rhode Island for at least one year…?"

"Yes." And I thought: Oh, much more than 12 months. It was 23 years ago that I brought the new wife to the starter house I'd purchased in Providence for $46,000. It's where I had been single, enjoying a young man's freedom. Not long after the wedding, I found myself on my own in Paris researching a book, and had an open night. Those had always been great times for me – being unattached and somewhere exotic. I had dinner at a small restaurant, browsed a bookstore, and later, stood on a bridge over the Seine in the shadow of Notre Dame. That's when it struck me that something was missing. I no longer enjoyed being alone. She had become part of me.

In time, I realized she even changed how I thought when I sat down to do my work. "You write for the one you love," Hemingway once said, and I had now begun to do that.

The magistrate looked on. The power to make this official was his. I was impressed to see sympathy on his face. Despite his years at this, he had not forgotten that it's always a sad moment.

"And you have three children together?" asked my lawyer.

"Correct," I said. And again I said no more. But I wanted to tell the judge how good we were as parents and partners. Yes, your honor, three children, the first a little girl – a girlie girl – and you should have seen me, a guy's guy lost in a house of pink things, sitting patiently as she put bows in my hair. Then came our first son, though we had trouble conceiving him to a point we felt it might not happen. But one afternoon, as I stood outdoors, my wife came from the house and looked me in the eye as only a wife does with a husband, and she told me it had happened. She was pregnant. A few years later, we had the youngest, another son, the only one mentioned by name here in the courtroom, because he is still a minor. If two children are from a small family, three make for a big one, and there began the richest years as my wife and I went from a man-to-man to a zone defense.

Suddenly, today, they were 22, 18 and 16, all on the brink of life on their own. Though the two of us often said we hoped they'd never fly too far.

Correct. We had three children together. And we always will.

Soon it was my wife's turn, and after she was done, we both sat with respective counsel at the plaintiff's and defendant's tables. We listened as the magistrate made it official… growing apart by the parties…different goals…cannot be reconciled…the court is satisfied.

And then it was over, the lawyers disappearing into the hallway in search of their next cases. We found ourselves leaving the building together, just the two of us.

It would be untrue to say this has been an easy year. Even in the best of divorces, there are hard times and resentments.

But right then, on the sidewalk outside the courthouse, we seemed to both find a moment of peace in this end of things. She thanked me, and I her. Separately, we walked toward our cars.

I felt I needed to somehow mark this, so I decided to take a detour. I drove to the two houses where we were together as a family. I passed by each address, and tried to feel what we once had.

Quickly, I continued on. I had a new home now, and a new life. It was time to begin it.

Dave Lieber now pens a column for the Dallas Morning News. Before that, he wrote for the Fort Worth Star-Telegram, where this column and the one that follows appeared. This piece ran October 2, 1994.

Dog's Not All I Need
To Fill Hole In My Life

Here in Texas, I've met the woman of my dreams. Unfortunately, she lives with the dog of my nightmares.

Karen, a woman I've known only six months, is calm and self-assured. A godsend. To me, she easily is the first Lady of Watauga. She lives in Watauga, is first in my life and is very much a lady.

Sadie, a Labrador retriever, is her dog. And she easily is the Last Dog of Watauga. She is last in my life and very much an obstacle. The Psycho Dog.

While Karen and her two children appear to love me very much. Psycho Dog hates and fears me.

The First Lady, who like me is divorced, rescued the Last Dog at age six months from an early life of apparent abuse – probably at the hands of some mean male. At age 2, Sadie is still skittish, hyperactive and impossible to deal with. Karen says the Last Dog is a lot like me.

But Sadie and I share the most important thing: We both love Karen with all the force of life. And we both gather strength from her thoughtful ways and tender hugs. If only the dog and I could get along.

The truth is, I didn't like Sadie. So how could she like me?

With Karen's two children, it didn't appear to matter that I have never been a father. We got along well from the start. No, Sadie was the problem. Karen says there's a hole in my life when it comes to animals, and filling that hole will make me whole.

Before our first date, Karen and I talked on the phone for hours. When I finally picked her up for a formal dinner in Grapevine, we felt like we'd known one another forever.

At the dinner, we sat with some top executives of this newspaper. A little nervous (well, a lot), I began the meal by spilling water on my editor. Not to be outdone, Karen dropped a pitcher of cream on the lap of my publisher. Knowing the embarrassment was now off me alone and shared by both of us, Karen turned and gave me a high-five. I knew then that it was love.

That's her style. From the start, we shared everything -- unless it was something that Karen could do better. Amazed that it took me three hours to mow my lawn, she bet $20 that she could do it in less than an hour. She clocked in at 49 minutes and 32 seconds.

Then one night, when I had a bad cold, Karen gently applied Vapor Rub to my chest – a daring act in this age of selfishness. In one stroke, she became my Florence Nightingale of Texas. "I don't want you to call me that," she said. "I want to be *Doctor Karen.*"

We both feel that the search of a lifetime is over; we've found each other. And her children appear to feel the same.

Jonathan, who is 10, longs for a stable father figure. He hugs me when he sees me, asks about my day and kisses me good night.

Desiree, who is 12, has opened my eyes to he world of hormones and mood swings that I never knew existed. And she has taught me the language of youth – her favorite expressions being, "Oh, I'm sure!" and "You're pathetic." She hugs me when she sees me and kisses me good night.

And what of Sadie? The runt of her litter, the Last Dog is half-sized, but she has big expressive eyes and a pretty white coat. Karen wanted me to get along with Sadie. Karen talked to me about compromise, about meeting Sadie halfway. I tried – to no avail.

Dog bones, canned meat and my special hamburgers didn't do the truck. Sadie ate them all – but showed me no gratitude.

When I called Sadie "Psycho Dog" to her face, Karen warned me to be careful. "She understands you." And Karen reminded me that filling the whole in my life would make me hole.

Finally, one day I decided to see the world through Sadie's eyes: I was a big, smelly brute who invaded her turf and came between her and her mother. A brute who didn't like her.

So that day, I sat down beside Sadie and told her I was sorry. Sorry for the way some man had apparently treated her. And sorry for how I hadn't shown her the proper understanding.

"I'll try to love you, Sadie," I said. "We're both lucky that Karen found us. I love you. I love you." I said it over and over. Those big expressive eyes looked up at me, and she licked my face.

Since that day, I always tell Sadie when I'm about to go – so as not to startle her. Karen says, "I'm glad you and Sadie have made peace."

But now I see the hole in my life needs more than just a dog to fill it. Karen, there's something magical about you, me, the girl, the boy – and even your doggone little dog.

I love you Karen. I'll always tell you when I'm about to go – so as not to startle you. And I promise to come back.

I'll always come back.

I want to stay forever. I really do.

Karen, will you marry me?

Postscript: Karen said yes. The couple married in February of 1995.

September 10, 2000

For Neighbors, Hateful Act Has Opposite Effect

So, punk, you come into my Park Glen neighborhood and break into a house and cover the walls with your filth by penning swastikas and misspelled slogans about blacks dying and going home, even though they already are home.

You deface the carpets, rip the linoleum, hammer holes into kitchen cabinets, tear up pillows and break glass frames that show Martin Luther King Jr., and a baby on whom you have so thoughtfully drawn a Hitler-like mustache.

The moment I hear, I dash over and knock on the Davises' front door and offer to help paint over your stupidity. Daniel and Rolanda Davis invite me in, and somebody asks, "Who's got paint trays?" So I rush out and get paint trays and tarpaulins, and I'm running across the store parking lot in a fury because I am on a mission to repair, repaint and rebuild everything you did so your act becomes as meaningless and wasted as possible.

I return to the house and meet the neighbors across the street, Marnie and Chris Pettit and David Polzin, and Brad Brittain, associate pastor of nearby Alliance United Methodist Church, and together we start painting over your evil and making each other laugh and bonding with neighbors I never knew in seven years of living in the neighborhood.

It dawns on me halfway through the afternoon, when the white paint is dripping down my arm and the paint fumes are starting to get to me and the sound of laughter in the house is so loud that the TV reporters downstairs are asking us to be quiet because it doesn't jibe with the solemn nature of the story they are trying to report, that what you have accomplished is exactly what you did not want to do.

I'm not talking about how you have proven yourself to be the dumbest of the dumb. I'm talking about how you unintentionally introduced us to this wonderful family who moved into our neighborhood a year ago and with whom we had never had the privilege of meeting.

We live in a world where people such as Daniel and Rolanda are the kind of people who are not only raising their two children, ages 8 and 14. They are so kind and so giving that they also are foster parents who share their love and hugs with children abandoned by others.

Truly amazing people.

We now know that Daniel, a mechanic for American Airlines, was a little startled several years ago when Rolanda broached the subject of opening up their home to foster children.

We know that when the first of many foster children entered their house – a 5-year-old girl named Mira, who felt scared and unloved – the Davis family scooped her up and changed her life forever. Mira learned to love and to hug and to kiss. When she eventually left for adoption and a permanent home, she was a happy girl.

"It just tugged at my heart," Daniel recalled.

He was so moved that he and his family could make a difference in the life of someone else that, from then on, he was hooked on helping the unwanted children of others. Such unselfish people in a selfish world.

Punk, last week when you broke in to their house and tromped from room to room, spilling red nail polish so it looked like blood and stabbing pillows with the fury of a madman, you invaded the fragile world of three foster children who need no more trauma in their young lives – a week-old baby, a month-old premature baby and an 18-month-old about to move to another home and start all over with a new mommy and daddy.

Were it not for Daniel and Rolanda, where would these little ones be?

So I'm standing in Daniel and Rolanda's bedroom, and I'm painting over your swastikas, retracing your madness again and again until the hate doesn't show on the walls any more.

Daniel walks by, sees the freshly painted walls and whispers, "All right. Excellent."

Marnie, the schoolteacher, and Chris, the auditor, are downstairs shielding the Davises from reporters like professional public relations people. Brad, the associate pastor, is upstairs telling me about how he wants to strangle you, punk, but he has learned such a valuable lesson that it has tempered his anger.

"I don't see a lot of hate in them," he says of Daniel and Rolanda. "I'm impressed with how they have handled this."

Punk, you failed in the biggest way.

Thank you for inadvertently introducing us to these beautiful people. What a privilege and an honor to meet them. I pray that your bigotry and hate do not drive them away. We cannot afford to lose such extraordinary neighbors.

Doug Moe currently writes a column for the Wisconsin State Journal. He penned this piece on October 19, 2006, for The Capital, Wis., Times.

Going Into Beast Mode

Gino got the lion from a farm couple in Columbia County.

"They were afraid that when he got big, he would eat the horses," Gino was saying this week.

The couple received the lion as an anniversary gift from their son, who was living in Texas. How the son acquired it is lost to history. But he hauled the lion up to Wisconsin, and after the parents took custody and the son was back in Texas, the ad went in the paper.

"Lion For Sale."

Gino, whose real name is John Uhalt, paid $500 for the cat. Around the same time, someone tried to sell him a baby elephant for $1,000, but Gino declined.

"What am I going to do with an elephant?" he said.

All this happened in 1979. News reports last weekend about a lion sanctuary in Sauk County running into zoning and permit problems prompted someone to ask Gino about his lion, which lives in Madison legend. On Tuesday, Gino sat in a booth in the Avenue Bar, spreading out old newspaper clippings and telling stories like a proud papa.

"He was pretty good with crowds," Gino said of the big cat, "though he had a short attention span."

When Gino first brought the lion to Madison, it took up a dual residency. Most days, it was at the sawmill that

Gino and his twin brother Jim operated near Chase Lumber in Sun Prairie, but once in a while they would bring the lion into Madison, where they owned a Rastafarian vegetarian restaurant, Friends Café, on Willy Street.

When Gino brought the animal to town, he was just a couple of months old. He was originally called Sphynx, a name Gino disliked, so he renamed him Sammy. Not too long after that, the name was changed again.

"We started calling him Big Sammy," Gino said.

By that time, the lion weighed 500 pounds. He could stand on his hind legs and take a hot dog off the rim of a basketball hoop.

"He was real affectionate," Gino said.

But like a lot of youngsters, Sammy could be rambunctious. In their living quarters at the sawmill, Gino and Jim noticed a series of small holes poked in all four walls of the living room.

"He was running around the living room without touching the floor," Gino said.

The Uhalts noted that in those days there were no laws against owning a lion, and they often took Sammy on field trips into Madison, where he was greeted like a rock star.

"When he showed up, he stopped the world," Jim said.

One day, Gino had Sammy on State Street. Hundreds of people gathered. That was after a visit to Jocko's, a bar just off State on Gilman. Entering Jocko's, Gino had tied Sammy's leash around a jukebox in the front of the bar. Gino then walked to the men's room in the back. When he returned, he found Sammy just outside the door. The lion had dragged the jukebox the length of the bar.

"He didn't know his own strength," Jim Uhalt said.

Over the years, Sammy broke all 14 windows in the sawmill. He would see the brothers out in the yard and wave at them with a paw. Goodbye, window. Sammy also liked to play tug-of-war with a long piece of rope or leather. It took four men on the other end to make it a contest. Yet when Gino tapped his nose, the lion would lie down on the ground.

One day, they took Sammy to the Vilas Zoo, which was probably a mistake. The other animals, the ones in cages, were lions.

The zoo management was not amused.

"And I do their trees," Gino said.

For a long time, he has operated a tree-trimming business in Madison. Gino and Jim are Madison natives, having graduated from Edgewood High School in 1963. Jim wound up getting a degree in economics at UCLA.

"The thing about taking him to the zoo," Jim said, "was that you could look in the eyes of the lions behind the bars, and they were empty, if you know what I mean. Sammy had those big, warm brown eyes."

In the mid 1980s, Sammy got sick with diabetes.

"He was born with it," Gino said.

He took Sammy to the vet, where he had been once before after Gino left him in the car too long and Sammy ate the front seat covers.

"Right down to the springs," Gino said.

Gino treated the diabetes with insulin, and Sammy rallied for a time. But he started slipping again, and this time he went quickly. Gino and Jim buried him near the sawmill.

"I was his guardian," Gino said, "and let me tell you, it was a full-time job."

Gino smiled.

"You should have heard him roar."

This Moe column ran on November 24, 2010, in the Wisconsin State Journal.

A Hunter's Comedy Of Errors

Sometimes you get the bear, sometimes the bear gets you, and sometimes you can't stop crying.

This episode from the wild kingdom also features a deer, a bow and arrow, and a hunter named Gary Spaeni, who spent 40 years in the woods without shooting a deer.

Last week, he did. At which point – in a fashion -- the bear got him. Tears followed.

Spaeni, 60, a retired Dane County social worker, is a familiar figure on local golf courses. He carries a single-digit handicap and, in 2007, appeared on a Golf Channel reality show called "Fore Inventors Only."

Spaeni had invented a cap with an enlarged and extended bill that – in the manner of putting blinders on a race horse – helps golfers focus on the ball.

He didn't win, but did earn a trip to Florida.

Spaeni is a less accomplished hunter than golfer, although he's not one of those guys who uses hunting as an excuse to drink and let his beard grow for a week.

He has a cabin in Florence County a couple hours north of Green Bay, and every fall he hunts both there and in Dane County. He uses a bow as well as a gun.

"I'm very poor at both," Spaeni was saying this week.

Yet he has hunted every season since 1970. He has failed every year, although there were times when he probably could have bagged a deer, but passed up the chance because he wanted a big trophy buck to be his first.

Lately, in part due to more complicated hunting regulations, Spaeni has grown less selective.

This year, he received one of only a few permits for archery hunting at the Jenni & Kyle Preserve, a park on Post Road in Madison. On Monday afternoon last week, he drove to the park and set up his metal ladder stand on the edge of some trees fronted by a marsh.

After an hour or so, Spaeni spotted a pair of antlerless deer about 50 yards away. He took aim and drew back his string, but the deer stopped behind a bush. When Spaeni could no longer hold his aim, he released the arrow and it sailed into the bush. The deer ran away. Ten minutes later, they were back. Spaeni shot again, missed and the deer fled.

Some time later, the deer – might they have heard of the man's 40-year record of failure – returned. It was nearly dark, and this time they were in the marsh. Spaeni fired and hit one of the deer, which took a few steps and collapsed.

It dawned on Spaeni that he didn't have the faintest idea what to do next. He didn't have a knife or even a flashlight.

"I never get anything," he said.

Spaeni drove home and shared the news with his wife, Sharon Fallon. He then watched an old VHS tape about how to field-dress a deer and headed back to the park.

In the black of night, he managed to find the deer and gut it.

"It was totally gross," he said. "I just wanted to come out with 10 fingers."

He took the deer to a hardware store to register it and then went home. Spaeni went back the next morning for his stand. With some difficulty, he fitted it into the back of his SUV and opened the driver's door.

Spaeni heard a hissing noise. For a moment, he thought he had a flat tire, but noticed a fog inside the car and suddenly he could neither see nor breathe.

"I was gagging and dying."

When Spaeni slammed the rear door, a piece of the deer stand punctured a can of Mace Bear Pepper Spray he had in his car to take up north for gun season.

He had Maced himself with bear repellent.

"I was completely incapacitated."

By early this week, the pepper spray still had not worked its way completely out of his system, or his vehicle.

Spaeni has been driving with the windows open and trying not to cry.

Still, Spaeni told me he was thinking of going hunting again later this week. It was hard to tell if he was serious or not. His eyes were filling with tears.

Colman McCarthy wrote this column for The Washington Post on September 23, 1989. These days, he directs the Center for Teaching Peace.

Some Telephone Word-Sleuthing With Robert Penn Warren

In a 1980 poem, Robert Penn Warren, who died at 84 on Sept. 15, used the word appallment. That was the first I had seen it. A look in the dictionary turned up appallingly, an adverb, but no appallment, a noun.

I phoned Warren at this home in Fairfield, Conn. His wife answered. When I explained the reason for my call, she let me know, politely, that with her standing guard over the time of one of the West's literary masters I'd have a better chance of getting through if I were selling vacation homes in Vladivostok. Besides, she and her husband were just going out and were already late. But thanks for calling.

Warren, perhaps putting on his rubbers in the foyer, overheard his wife. From the mufflings, she had put her hand over the receiver. No doubt practiced in dispatching pests and groupies, she was likely waving him off with the other hand.

It didn't work. Moments later, Warren came on. His voice – soft, drawling, restful – reminded me of his southern-life novels that I had read 20 years before, and some of his poems, too, such as "Boyhood in Tobacco Country." For a few generous minutes, Warren talked about appallment, speaking like a gourmet chef over a kettle happy to spoon flavorings of some fresh-simmering vocabulary. He knew the word wasn't in the dictionary, he said, but piffle: "If you're writing and a word is needed, you create it. This is a word that ought to exist. I've invented other words. Appallment is my latest."

I remember not doing anything useful the rest of the day, so deep was the reverie of talking with Robert Penn Warren about language. It was like being a sandlot kid calling up Joe DiMaggio for his ideas on hitting. "What is man but his passion?" Warren asks in the first lines of "Audubon: A Vision," with his own passionate commitment to precise and soaring words ensuring that his poems stood, as he hoped, "as a vital emblem of the integrity of the self."

Unlike the best of Warren's novels – beginning with the 1946 "All the King's Men" – in which the essential material was plot and characters, his poems relied on "some kind of vital image…That's a different thing from the vitality you observe or experience. It's an image of it, but it has the vital quality, rather than a passing reflection, but it has its own kind of life, by the way it's built."

Warren's usage represented a digging for preciseness, of expressing the writer's integrity of serving the reader. In the preface to his dictionary, Samuel Johnson said, "Write without effort, and they read it without pleasure." Warren, dogged in spending effort on the right word, said it another way: "A lot of current can come through a small wire."

As it did, in the electricity of such adjectives as gracility and instancy and such verbs as unspool. He

likes words ending, as did appallment, in m-e-n-t:
enchainment, embracement. Once he came up with the
word unwordable.

> *You dream that somewhere, somehow, you may*
embrace
> *The world in its fullness and threat, and feel,*
like Jacob, at last
> *The merciless grasp of unwordable grace*
> *Which has no truth to tell of future or past.*

The purity of Warren's language came from his lack of
interest in much else. "I've been a lot of places," he said,
"and done a lot of things, but writing was always first.
It's a kind of pain I can't do without. It's not a
particularly fun way to live. It's just scratching where
you itch. But it's my life."

Some of Warren's poems were metaphysical, and
others were complex in their cumulative enlargements of
image. He liked to assure beginning writers, as well as
students, that a poem's inspiration has birth in the
ordinary: "You don't write poems sitting at a typewriter,
you write them swimming or climbing a mountain or
walking." Another time he said, "Lines, verses, even
stanzas, come to me at odd moments – perhaps the best
when I'm swimming. Swimming frees the mind. There's
something about the rhythm of swimming – or running.
The body is occupied, and the mind is free."

So, too, are politics. In 1930, Warren joined other
southern intellectuals to produce "I'll Take My Stand," a
pitch for reactionary bromides about race. A quarter-
century later, his liberalism surfaced in "Segregation: the

Inner Conflict in the South" followed by "Who Speaks for the Negro?" in 1965.

Warren resisted the role that tempts so many heirs of the Confederacy, that of the professional southerner ever explaining the region to the rest of the world. He lived in New England, for one thing, and his breadth was larger than a geography. He believed that a person who reads a piece of writing is "establishing a relationship" with the author "through the medium," and both become "part of the human community."

That's why the phone call was a thrill. Warren's poems had long spoken to me, and now he had. On a small wire, current came through.

June 22, 1991

Help The Homeless, But Not Here

A pattern seems to be developing in the life and work of Michael Kirwan. People praise him for his love of humankind but, please, they say, do it elsewhere.

Since a winter evening in 1978 when he brought a bowl of soup to a man freezing on a heat vent near the State Department, Kirwan has been sharing his considerable energies with destitute people who have no homes and no one to turn to but him. In 1978 he was in his mid-20s and a graduate student at George Washington University. Homelessness was not yet a national issue; social workers and nuns, the local Mother Teresas, were expected to deal with it. Kirwan asked himself, "Why not me?" and began opening up his university-owned apartment to several men living on the street.

When school officials said his dormitory was not a shelter, Kirwan refused to leave. "For the first time in my life," he recalled, "I took a stand. I told them I wouldn't leave until all of us had a place to go. The university took me to court. The judge was very sympathetic and told me that what I was doing was a good thing, but that I couldn't do it in university housing. He told me, though, that he would give me three months to find another place to live and that we could all stay together."

Kirwan did find a place. And another and another. Today he lives with poor people in a three-story brick row house in a poor neighborhood that lies midway between the U.S. Capitol and Mt. Pleasant, the area that erupted this spring. Once again, with as many as 300 people coming in daily for meals, clothes and a place to rest and be listened to, Kirwan is being told that he's the right person in the wrong place.

Real-estate speculators have been investing in the neighborhood, turning the shabby into the sparkling. Eyesore row houses have been renovated into residential jewels, including two properties next door to Kirwan's home. In May, a subway stop opened a block away, a civic improvement that will further push up property values and push out the already displaced.

The pressures on Kirwan to move along are the same seen elsewhere, when either public officials or neighborhood associations decide that homeless people are menaces to progress or tranquility. In New York last week, 30 homeless people were routed from an encampment under the West Side Highway. They are blocking a road-improvement project. The 13 wooden shacks, which the New York Post called "relatively fancy," were set up a year ago when police removed a group of homeless people from nearby Riverside Park.

In Atlanta, the country's latest anti-panhandling law is being strictly enforced. Sidewalk begging is being criminalized the way it has been in other cities. It is constitutional – still – to stand on a street corner with a tin cup, but it isn't if passersby are asked to drop in a quarter.

In the 1980s much of the country responded positively to the needs of homeless people. The response now is turning negative. Instead of reaching out, kick them out. At his current residence, into which he moved in 1985 when a McLean physician gave him a large donation to buy the house, Michael Kirwan's troubles began two years ago. He had an emergency and called a fire department ambulance. It was noticed that too many people were living in the house: "We had to get a certificate of occupancy after five different inspections. I didn't know what a certificate of occupancy was, and our house had never been inspected at all. Now it is a running battle and concern that they will try to shut us down."

When inspectors show up and see the kitchen and living room astir with people eating dinner, Kirwan is told that he can't run a soup kitchen in his neighborhood. He replies that he's not; he's sharing a meal with friends. When the officials look upstairs and see beds packed into rooms and mattresses on the floor, he's told he can't run a shelter. He answers that he's not; this is his house, these are his guests and he believes in hospitality.

Grumbles have been heard in the neighborhood. It is being asked, Who gave Kirwan permission? No one, he answers: "I simply moved in, and people moved in with me…There is nothing to fear. We are human beings helping other human beings, and isn't that what our lives are all about?"

Kirwan enjoys reading the lives of the saints, which further confuses people. One of his favorites is the Spanish mystic, St. John of the Cross. "He said one time," Kirwan recalls, "that in the twilight of our lives we will be judged on love, that's all. Not what we accumulated, or what power or prestige we had, or that we gave lots of money or things. Just simply on how we loved…What else is there?"

If any housing inspectors, judges, road-improvement officials, real-estate speculators or neighbors have an answer, Michael Kirwan would like to hear it. So would his houseguests.

Ben Beagle is retired from the Roanoke, Va., Times. This column ran on September 12, 1975.

No Longer A Passing Fancy

"There comes a time in the affairs of all men where there is no small boy around the backyard to catch passes," said this friend of mine who takes everything very seriously.

"That is true," I said. "Small boys who used to catch fatherly, crisp spirals in the back yard have now all turned into people who are massive human beings. They can be observed frequently with their heads under the hoods of various old automobiles. When they are not occupied in this manner, they are chasing girls."

The man who takes everything seriously gazed for a long time at the mountains to the west. There was a nice September wind. But it did not cheer him.

"I came across a football a small boy used to catch, or drop, just the other day," he said. "It was stuffed and time had leaked the air out of it. It was like looking at the past."

The September wind turned cold, almost tomb-like, and I watched the western mountains, too.

"There is nothing that will make a man realize his mortality like a stuffed football, dead in the corner of what used to be a small boy's closet," I said.

"I would give anything to throw a forward pass to a small boy again," the man who is serious about everything said. "When the weather is like this, everything within me cries to throw a forward pass to a small boy in the back yard."

He looked mournful there in the back yard, his old sneakers on and the fingers of his right hand gripped, briefly, a phantom football that was clean and new, unscuffed and rigid with air.

"Where have all the boys who used to catch, or drop, backyard passes gone?" he asked.

"They have gone under car hoods and after girls," I said. "They have gone to be deafened by stereo music played too loud. They have reached the river and they are trying to cross and strange juices are flowing. They will not come again, I am afraid."

"I tried throwing passes at a peach basket the other day," the man said. "It was no fun. I tried throwing passes to a 9-year-old girl, but it was no fun. She is not interested in catching fatherly passes. She is interested in reading 'Black Beauty.' She has read it three times. She does not have the hands, either."

"I tried a peach basket, too," I said, becoming more sharply aware of mortality. "But you can't argue with a peach basket when it drops a pass. You can't teach a peach basket that the secret is in the fingertips."

A van painted in outrageous colors raced down the street. It was loaded with boys who were once small and caught, or dropped, forward passes in back yards. Instead of dropping forward passes, they are now dropping transmissions on perilous streets and roads.

"I am going to saddle soap that old ball," the man who takes everything seriously said. "I am going to saddle soap it and recapture the past."

He was pleased and ran off jauntily in his sneakers. He will not recapture the past. Mere saddle soap will not do this. The past had just gone by in the painted van.

January 8, 1981

Chain Saw Wars: A Forgettable Day In The Field

Here is the aging, semi-hysterical reporter in the realm and bosom of nature – 10-inch chain saw in hand and vast mountain ridges striding behind him in the cold January morning.

Here is the aging, semi-hysterical reporter's son, who is neither aging nor semi-hysterical. He has a 14-inch saw.

We are about man's work this day, and for this reason, one supposes, we have brought along an editor with a 14-inch saw. Editors with 14-inch chain saws are formidable people, and it is a comfort to have one along on this day made for the sturdy work of woodcutting.

A dusting of snow lies prettily on the ridges and in the hollows, and we observe our own breath in the air. We are men of purpose and dignity, invoking anew the pioneer spirit, stalwart ancestors no doubt watching these efforts with ancient approval.

I have on my L.L. Bean boots, my L.L. Bean thermal socks, my well-worn Wranglers, my well-worn L.L. Bean shirt, a blue turtleneck and my Jeep cap. I am wondering if there are any fashion photographers around. My hopes and ego are high.

We begin and disaster occurs in this pleasant Botetourt County setting.

The son's chain saw refuses to start again after cutting two pieces from a downed tree – the species of which none of us can imagine.

He will spend the next two hours in vain pulling on the starter.

The editor and I begin our manly assault on a downed apple tree, and it is not long before the editor discovers that the bar on his saw is inadequate. We can tell this because the saw cuts in circles – a trait that is admired in home workshop saws being used to make charming little corner shelves, but maddening to an editor cutting wood to keep the fireside snug and warm.

The editor and the son are soon stomping about this pastoral setting in moods that are often natural to both of them.

My little 10-inch saw is cutting into the apple wood, and I am pausing periodically to deliver clever, brief dissertations on the nobility of this wood, how it will glow in the stove and keep us warm.

The gentle people who have allowed us on this property stop by to watch, and they are very kind in their comments – even as I discover that I have allowed the chain on my saw to become slack enough to dull its teeth, perhaps permanently.

Now, we are without any saws at all, but the son, who can fix most things, transfers the spark plugs from the disabled editor's saw to his own and it begins to rattle and echo against the ridges. In the interim, he has also given me a lecture on how one checks from time to time on the tension in the chain. Soon he is cutting down a sycamore tree.

The gentle people who have allowed three miscreants of varying ages on their property are watching him with perfectly concealed dismay as the sycamore comes crashing down on their barbed wire fence – the result of a miscalculation in the physics of which way trees fall.

They smile tolerantly, and I am very glad that no photographers of any kind showed up for this one. My Wranglers are a mess anyway and my turtleneck has rolled unattractively under my chins.

The gentle people do not call the sheriff, and we load our wood and leave.

That night, I dream of chain saws and ill-felled sycamores. The next day I wear my Leggett corduroys and warm sweater as I watch the Dallas Cowboys luck out again. When I go out for wood at the end of the first quarter, I hear a faraway chain saw. "Poor chap," I say.

3
RUNS
&
A VAN

This column by the late Mike Harden appeared in the Columbus, Ohio, Dispatch on May 7, 1997. Harden died of cancer in 2010. He was 64.

I've Got The Moving Day Blues

I am moving at the end of this month. I would rather bungee-jump into the settling tank at a sewage treatment facility, but I have little choice and less Valium.

My father so loathed moving that, the few times our family did, he insisted it be done while he was at work.

"Just call the shop with the address when you get settled," he would instruct my mother.

The act of moving is enchanting only to the hopelessly deranged. The reason California boasts the highest per-capita rate of certifiable lunatics is that most of them are spawn of the toxic gene pool of "movers" who settled the state.

Those who ended up in California so loved moving that they spent months of it on the trail West. Some got typhoid or tomahawked and left their bones to bleach in Death Valley. Their idea of fun was to become snowbound in a mountain pass with all their belongings on a wagon, and then to survive until spring by cannibalizing the frozen bodies of in-laws.

My chief beef with the process of relocating can be summed up with an oxymoron: professional movers.

I have never seen a "professional mover." I usually get three guys named Snake, Cooter and Mongo, along with their probation officer.

These are guys with pierced eyebrows and Metallica tattoos who first bonded during group therapy in prison and have stayed together to network toward mutual long-term goals.

If I were casting them in a movie, I'd get Nicolas Cage, Steve Buscemi and Michael J. Pollard.

Of course, I'd never get the real Cage, Buscemi and Pollard. The three I usually get have appeared on film only in bank security cameras.

They arrive an hour late, driving a truck emblazoned with the logo for Walleye Sam's Seafood. They explain that they picked up the vehicle for a song a week earlier after its refrigeration unit failed while carrying 15,000 pounds of perch down from Lake Erie.

It smells like the kitchen exhaust fan at Long John Silver's.

It is folly to expect that men who have been eating off metal trays for the past 2-to-5 would have much respect for the china of total strangers. Remember the apes in the Samsonite commercial?

I try to accommodate the movers with small talk, though it often takes unsettling turns:

"Nice place. You folks got a security system?"

"No. No yet."

"Ought to. Someone could come out of those woods and strip this place clean in, oh, maybe nine minutes. Nearest police substation is 10 minutes away."

"You think so?"

"Sure. See these window locks on the side of your house that's hidden by the bushes from the road? Pop those babies in two seconds."

I try to keep things vague when it comes to professional movers. It helps little that I'm married to an obsessive-compulsive.

I label boxes: "Dining room stuff."

She labels them: "Waterford crystal" and "Coin collection: 19th-century $20 gold pieces."

Another problem with movers is that no matter how thoroughly you try to prepare for their arrival, they always manage to find something from Frederick's that fell behind the dryer.

This you discover after Mongo bellows, "Hey, Snake! Cooter! Check this out. Looks like a swimming cap for a guy with a Mohawk."

I'd just as soon burn down the house and all the packed boxes in it and start fresh.

Yet I know that, several days from now, I will be seated at my dining room table at sunset of a very long day looking at Snake, Cooter and Mongo, hearing:

"It's, uh, $1,100, dude. That don't include no tip or nothing, which is up to you."

I will tip, wave goodbye and call the home-security sales rep.

September 20, 1998

World's Oldest Columnist
Makes The Words Flow

"How old are you?" Rose Nix Leo asked, after an amiable phone chat about our mutual calling -- the column-writing business.

"Fifty-two," I replied.

"You've got a long way to go," she observed, chuckling at the realization that she is twice my age and still churning out a weekly column for the Elk County Citizen-Advance News in southeastern Kansas.

She wrote her first column at 17, the year Ronald Reagan was born, the year before the Titanic went down.

She remembers well the subject of that maiden effort.

"Dead Man's Gulch," she recounted. "There was a tree there that they used to hang criminals. They hung 'em there and buried 'em there. There were several graves.

"The law wasn't like it is now. People took it in their own hands and did the punishing. No trial. No lawyers."

It was a different Kansas into which Leo was born 104 years ago.

She was only 4 when her father was kicked to death by a horse. Three years later, her mother suffered a heat stroke while picking cotton and died several days later.

Relatives reared the five Nix children.

Rose only finished one year of high school, but that was enough to land her a teaching job at a one-room rural school in 1918.

"The first year I taught, I got $35 a month and I paid $10 for room and board."

She didn't quit the column, although her initial efforts were rewarded only with a sheaf of writing paper, enough postage for the next column, and the lofty title "county correspondent."

"I just started writing local news," she said. "Who went where. What they did. I've advanced a lot since then."

She married John Leo in 1920. He farmed, but the drought, dust and Depression made for a precarious existence in the 1920s and '30s.

"In '36," she recalled, "the corn was about two feet high, the gardens burned up and the grasshoppers took everything."

She sold her column to any editor who would have it, grateful for the pocket change it provided to help put food on the table for three growing children.

Her oldest son went off to fight in World War II. Seriously wounded in the South Pacific, he did not live long after he was returned to the States.

A daughter and another son remain.

Her husband died in 1967. At that time, she was writing a column for the Citizen titled "Rose's Last Scrap."

"I read in the Bible that after Jesus fed the multitudes, He said, 'Pick up every last scrap of food'. I decided that I'd write about every different thing, about the last scraps."

It is about friends, reminiscences, the changing seasons, the transactions of nature in the garden she yet tends.

Some years ago, she wrote about a bag of seeds she discovered near the lumberyard in Howard. She planted them in her garden and used the five-pointed compound leaf the plant produced in her flower arrangements.

"I took some to church," she said. "They looked awful pretty.

"It was marijuana."

She wrote about it, of course. By then, the plants were more than six feet tall.

A couple of interlopers sneaked into her garden one night after the column appeared and made off with her crop.

Lately, she has been sticking to sweet potatoes.

When asked how she writes her column, she replied tersely, "I write it with my right hand. I have an easy chair and a 300-watt reading lamp. I've got a pad to write on, and that's it. I send it longhand, and they type it at the paper."

Although no one has actually certified that she is, indeed, the oldest working columnist in the country, she doesn't hesitate when asked about that distinction.

"You don't have to look any farther."

It's a title she plans to keep a while longer.

"As long as my brain will function," she said, "and when it doesn't I don't even care to be here."

Three days from deadline, she was still pondering possible topics for the next "Rose's Last Scrap."

"I don't know. I'll think of something. My basket isn't empty."

Maggie Van Ostrand is a freelance writer and columnist. She was head writer for the game show, "Trivia Trap." This piece appeared on May 9, 2005.

What About A Nobel Prize For Motherhood?

A beautiful woman is queen of every room she enters. Conversation hushes, people turn to look, and the center of attention falls upon her. My mother was not like that. She was ordinary, quiet, and far more comfortable in a flowered print apron than in a little black dress. Yet, to us, she was the most beautiful woman in the world.

She was the queen of our house, could answer every question, and was a star in my father's eyes. How she managed such excellent meals on the shoestring budget she allowed herself is beyond me. Sure, we had a lot of spaghetti, but the kids loved spaghetti and so did our dad.

Mom was the most knowledgeable person in all things because she read every newspaper published in New York and, in those days, there were an awesome lot of them. She knew baseball stats back to the beginning of the sport, and what prizefighter knocked out what other prizefighter, and the year he did it. She knew all the politicians, local and national, current and historical, and all kinds of international news. She was an avid reader of books, made most of our clothes and could knit and crochet with the best of them.

Dad used to boast that when he wore a pair of socks she had darned, he couldn't even feel the stitches. She kept the family checkbook balanced and did the taxes. And still, she managed to save enough to send small sums to her favorite charities, and even enough to buy us pretty Easter outfits.

Mom always managed to hide the eyes she had in the back of her head, the ones she never tired of warning us about. Hindsight indicates that we took for granted a clean home, delicious meals, and nothing to worry about (as long as we passed all our grades). Until we became moms ourselves, we never realized the balancing act it took to pay the bills, run a smooth house, and not expect any credit, just results. There should be a Nobel Prize for Motherhood.

Even thought a beautiful woman can conquer a roomful of strangers, it takes a mother to conquer a family full of life.

May 11, 2007

Unknown To Most, But
A Hero Just The Same

Until yesterday, I had never heard of Charlie Foster. Today, I'm writing about him. One of the benefits of being a writer is the fact-checking, because you can end up with provocative information. That's how I found out about Charlie Foster.

An ace flier is defined as a fighter pilot who destroyed five or more enemy aircraft. Charlie was a World War II ace with the 201st Fighter Squadron. What's more, his heroism beyond the call of duty netted him a Congressional Medal of Honor.

Yet no one made a movie about Charlie Foster, the way they did about Audie Murphy, the Medal of Honorwinning hero in "To Hell and Back." No HBO miniseries about Charlie was made by Tom Hanks and Steven Spielberg the way they made "Band of Brothers" about the Second World War's 101st Airborne Division's Easy Company. No Hollywood studio made an Oscar-winning film about the 201st, as they did about the Civil War's first all-black volunteer company in 1989's "Glory."

But in its way, Charlie's tale is as special as those famous stories of heroic actions. His real name isn't Charlie Foster. It's Carlos Faustinos and he was a Mexican citizen. Carlos fought beside American airmen in the Pacific Theater and was a member of the elite "Esquadron Aereo de Caza 201," also known as the Fighting 201st.

Not only did this information surprise me, but so did the fact that Mexico declared war on the Axis Powers on June 11, 1942. Imagine that. Can't you just see kind, agricultural Mexico declaring war on the Big Bad Wolves Hirohito, Mussolini and Hitler? But Mexico did indeed declare war, and they put their men where their collective mouth was.

Mexico organized the 201st Fighter Squadron, a select group of pilots that included Carlos Faustinos. Thirty-five officers and 300 enlisted men were trained in Mexico, then given additional flight training as P-47 fighter squadron at Pocatello Army Air Base in Idaho, and were then attached to the 58th Fighter Group in the Philippines, where they began combat operations. The unit wiped out machine gun nests, dropped 181 tons of bombs and fired 153,000 rounds of ammunition, acquitting themselves bravely. Seven of their pilots were killed in action.

The Fighting 201st wasn't the only heroic group of Mexicans. In a town called Silvis, just west of Chicago, runs a street once named Second Street. It's not much of a street, not even two blocks long, muddy in spring, icy in winter, dusty in summer. On this single street, 105 men participated in World War II, Korea and Vietnam. It's the street where Joe Gomez, Peter Macias, Johnny Munos, Tony Pompa, Claro Soliz and Frank, Joseph and William Sandoval grew up together. They worked for the railroad, like their fathers who had emigrated from Mexico. These young men, raised to revere freedom, went to war without hesitation.

The two Sandoval families alone sent 13 to the front. According to the Defense Department, this little street contributed more men to military service than any other place of comparable size in the United States, standing alone in American military history.

In a letter to Frank Sandoval, Claro Soliz described Second Street as "…really not much, just mud and ruts, but right now to me it is the greatest street in the world." He never saw it again. Not one of these boys came home alive.

In honor of their sacrifice, a monument listing the name of each man now stands in Silvis, Ill. Second Street has been officially renamed Hero Street USA.

Maybe their stories weren't sensational enough to be covered by CNN, but they happened just the same.

Jerry Zezima has written a humor column for the Stanford, Conn., Advocate since 1985. His books include "Leave It to Boomer." This piece appeared March 24, 2013.

Grandparenting Tips From Poppie

Now that I am a grandfather, many people whose children have recently had children have asked for my brilliant advice on how to be a good grandparent. As a world-renowned expert whose granddaughter is not even two months old but is already more mature than I am, I'd be happy to comply.

For new grandparents, changing diapers is the No. 1 concern. It's also, of course, the No. 2 concern. But more on that later.

First, you should know that my precious little pumpkin is the most beautiful grandbaby ever born. It is important to acknowledge this and to stop thinking that your grandchild is more adorable than mine. He or she may have been the most beautiful before my granddaughter made her grand entrance into the world, but not any more. Sorry, but that's just the way it is.

With that settled, here is a vital grandparenting tip: Don't brag. Nobody wants to listen to you babble on about how alert, wonderful and beautiful your grandchild is while looking at 100 photos you have just taken of the little cutie. Fifty photos are more than enough.

Yes, you are proud to be a grandparent, but a little humility goes a long way. You might say something like, "My grandbaby isn't as alert, wonderful and beautiful as Jerry Zezima's, but then, whose grandchild is?"

This brings me to your interaction with the baby. As a grandparent, you will have a profound influence on your grandchild for better (as in the case of my wife, Sue, also known as Nini) or for worse (as in the case of yours truly, also known as Poppie).

As evidence of this, I have already babysat for my granddaughter a few times. I fed her, changed her and played with her. I also watched baseball and hockey games with her. I even told her jokes while I held her. She looked up at me and smiled. When her mommy heard this, she said, "That was just gas."

Now we come to the crucial part: caring for the baby. It may have been 30 years since you were last entrusted with an infant, but it will all come back to you in pungent waves of nostalgia.

As you will recall, babies do three things: sleep, eat and poop. Nice work if you can get it.

The main difference between babies and adults is that babies not only can get away with it, but are actually praised for their efforts.

"Yay!" is the typical reaction when the baby polishes off a bottle faster than you have ever chugged a beer.

"Good job!" everyone says when the baby burps.

"Way to go!" they all exclaim, coughing slightly, when the baby does his or her business.

Speaking of which, being on diaper duty is not nearly as bad as it seemed when your kids were babies. In fact, it's a refreshing change. Well, maybe not refreshing, but it's breathtakingly simple, even if it's not a good idea to breathe while cleaning up.

This helps you bond with your grandchild and is the ultimate proof of your love and devotion to the little darling.

There you have it, new grandparents. This is just a primer, and I will impart more wisdom to you as your grandchild gets older, but at least now you have the basics.

So go ahead and enjoy being a Nini or a Poppie. There's nothing like it. You can even brag a little. You can also feel free to show unsuspecting people all those pictures you just took because I know that the new addition to your family really is beautiful.

And don't forget the most important thing. Despite what anyone says, when your adorable little grandbaby smiles at you, it's not necessarily gas.

July 22, 2011

When In Paris…Pardon My French

I'll always have Paris.

Excusez-moi, s'il vous plait. I should say. I'll always have Paris-Charles de Gaulle Airport, where I recently spent eight minutes (*huit minutes*) sprinting from one airplane (*l'avion*) to another during an otherwise magnificent (*magnifique*) and memorable (*memorable*) trip to France (*la France*).

My wife (*ma femme*), Sue (*Sue*) and I (*Jerry*) flew from New York to Boston, where we had a layover of more than five hours (*cinq heures*) before crossing the Atlantic (*Atlantique*) to Paris and then, after our mad dash through the airport to catch our connecting flight, which was boarding as we were landing, to our final destination, Marseille (no translation).

It was during this interminable journey that I completely mastered the French language (*francais*). Using a book titled "Say It in French," I memorized key French phrases (*Ou sont les toilettes*? Where is the men's room?) and words (*au secours*! help!), then practiced saying them with a nasally intonation that would have sounded better if I'd had a head cold.

Unfortunately, I fell asleep during the last hour of the transatlantic flight and forgot most of it, though I managed to get by without insulting anyone, which might have gotten me in trouble with the police (*gendarmes*).

Fortunately, and contrary to their unfair reputation for being rude, the French people were extremely pleasant (*agreable*) and helpful (*utiles*).

Whenever I didn't know what I was saying, which I can do in any language, I would ask, "*Parlez-vous anglais?*" (Do you speak English?") The very nice person who knew I was a fumbling American (*americain*) would smile, hold his or her thumb and forefinger an inch from each other and respond, "A little beet."

Then that person would proceed to speak English with a charming French accent. To show my gratitude, I would speak English with a terrible French accent.

This came in handy when our luggage (*les bagages*) showed up two days after we did. I consulted my little phrase book for the proper reaction (not repeatable in either language) after being forced to wear the equivalent of a prison-issue T-shirt that was kindly provided by the airline. You don't know what a thrill it is on your first visit to a foreign country to wear the same underwear (*les sous-vetements*) for 48 hours.

My mastery of French also came in handy when eight of the nine people in our party got violently ill. The sole exception was me (*moi*). It was not because of the food. *Au contraire*! The meals we had in France were delicious (*delicieux*). Rather, somebody caught a stomach bug that passed from one person to the next until the toilette almost exploded.

"*Je suis pas malade*" (I am not ill"), I told Bruno who, with his lovely wife, Gielle, owns Hostellerie du Luberon, where we stayed.

"*Pourquoi?*" (Why?") he asked.

"*Vin rouge*" ("Red wine"), I explained.

"Ha ha!" ("*Ha ha!*") Bruno laughed. "You have French blood!"

When everyone was feeling better, we went sightseeing. The South of France is like rural New England, with its rolling green (*vert*) hills and farms. Vineyards (see: *vin rouge*, above) are everywhere.

I especially enjoyed the markets in Luberon and Cadenet, where I purposely stood in people's way just so I could say – in French, of course – "pardon" ("*pardon*").

One day Sue and I got into our rented car (*la voiture*) and took a day trip to Aix-en-Provence, where we got lost thanks to the annoying woman whose voice, in English, was programmed into our GPS (Gallic Positioning System).

Her (for the 150th time): "Recalculating."

Me: "*Taisez-vous!*" ("Shut up!")

All in all, however, our trip was fantastic (*fantastique*). France is a beautiful country with wonderful people. Next time we go, we'll see more of Paris than just the airport.

Vive la France! Merci beaucoup. And, to anyone who was within earshot when our language got lost, pardon my French.

Donna Britt is the author of "Brother and Me: A Memoir of Loving and Giving." She was a nationally syndicated columnist for The Washington Post. This column appeared March 8, 1994.

Please, Muffy, Shut The Hell Up

This might have been a perfectly good column. I had the idea, the reasoning, the surprising insights all nailed. You woulda loved it.

But I got distracted again. By her.

Despite the years she's been with me, I've never seen her face. She has no name that I know of. I suspect there are millions like her.

She – let's call her Muffy – is the white voice inside my head.

No, I'm not one of those folks you see roaming the streets, chatting with unbidden demons. My bigoted inner voice – which has the nerve to claim it speaks for practically all of white America – is my own creation.

That doesn't make it any easier to shut her up.

Muffy speaks to me in whispers, murmurs and shouts. She waits until I am weary or vulnerable to do her worst. She knows never to let up on her ugliness.

"White people will never accept you," my voice whispers. "No matter how many of us may pretend otherwise, we believe we are better than you."

Sometimes I hear Muffy after reading a crime story in which the perpetrator is black. The voice – my in-house spokesperson for millions of whites – snorts, "That's what you people do." Or if a TV news story focuses on public assistance and the face on the screen is black, she sniffs, "Just like your kind. Why should I pay to support you?"

I hate her. Because even when I know I'm OK, no better or worse than anyone else, she speaks for those who'll never be convinced.

Some African-Americans never hear such voices. Sometimes, I'm just not that evolved. At those moments, Muffy – always judging, testing, pushing – gets to me. Like when I fall or stumble and she rants that I've disappointed millions of African-Americans, never just myself.

I only recently learned how old she is. The great black scholar W.E.B. DuBois wrote about the "double-consciousness" of American black people nearly a century ago in his classic book, "The Souls of Black Folks."

My, how things haven't changed.

In some ways, black Americans' limiting inner voices are like those heard by every human – voices that tell us we aren't rich, beautiful or educated enough, that our extra pounds somehow lessen us.

Black people have as many of those everyday-draining voices as anyone. Add this extra, awful one, and often, it's one voice too many. And although I know the voice goads many black people to "I'll-show-you" excellence in every field, it drives others to a "Why try?" despair.

My own personal, negative chorus showed up in the early 1960s after I realized, at age 6, that the people on TV getting dogs sicced on them down South looked like me. Once I figured out that the only "colored" people I saw in popular culture were maids in movies, singers or athletes – never, ever the craftsmen, teachers, doctors

and regular kids I saw and knew – I reached a
conclusion: Whites see blacks as being fundamentally
less. Sometimes I wondered if we really were less.

Otherwise, I asked, where was the wonderful stuff that
celebrated me? I decided "they" hated me.

And I met Muffy, who made sure I'd never forget.

Even before adulthood, some real people challenged
her: friendly white kids at the junior high school I was
bused to; and Brenda, a co-worker at my first high
school job, who invited me to a party at her home – an
unheard-of thing in 1970s Indiana.

But always, another ugly glance or news event brought
Muffy back.

Black people's lifelong exposure to the ways of whites,
through every facet of culture, means we know them in
under-the-skin ways, understand them as most whites –
with little authentic entrée into black communities –
can't know us.

What's dangerous about our knowledge is that
however well we know white people, we can't know it
all. However schooled we are in racism's history and
omnipresence, we can't always know when individuals
are motivated by it. Our voices are based on real
experiences, but in themselves are not real.

So even though Muffy often is useful, I wish she'd shut
the hell up.

She wears me out. I asked a close white friend who
works with black people if she has a similar voice, a
black one. "No," she said slowly. "The only thing I have
that's remotely comparable is a voice that tells me I can't
possibly know what it's like being black. Even when I'm

tempted to think so. But nothing that dogs me…" Of course not.

So what if, at times, blacks need cautionary voices? Like in 1955 Mississippi, where a warning whisper might have told Emmett Till, 14 – who'd been raised up north to act like he was equal – never to flirt white. His murderers later said how shocking it was, that this boy had so little fear before they lynched him.

But I want a rest from Muffy's hatred and pessimism. I'm sick of how, for all her on-target accusations, she never prepares me for white people's goodness, for the support I've received from them.

Of course, white racists are out there – I hear from them. But considering the negative chorus inside my head, the last thing I need is naysaying within.

Why give any voice not my own that much power?

So listen up, Muffy: I'm handing you your eviction papers. Kicking you to the curb. You heard me – get out, goodbye and good riddance.

What's that? You won't go?

You hate this column? You're sick of my whining? And – hey, hold it a minute.

Could you at least turn down the volume?

Finding Love In Furry, Doggone Places

Christmas is no time for your dog to die.

Even if you despise him.

Thirteen years ago, I wrote a controversial column about Silverado, the American Eskimo whom my son Darrell, then 7, chose as a pet from owners who swore that the bouncy 6-month-old was "mostly housebroken." White and bubbly as a tub of suds and with eyes like shiny black marbles, Silverado was utterly beautiful – and half as bright as any of the fleas that soon infested our house and left no inch of me unbitten.

The column's controversy? I admitted that I hated him.

Silverado had shredded my every piece of expensive lingerie, defecated repeatedly on my white carpet and eaten an entire bottle of Flintstones vitamins before barfing in Technicolor.

Despite his placid, beauty-queen face, Silver was, as I wrote in 1992, a 25-pound roller coaster ride: "Give him the slightest provocation – like breathing – and he becomes Tasmanian Devil Dog: panting, jumping, licking, spinning, nipping, whining and slobbering all at once."

The mailman quaked before his snapping jaws; casual friends reconsidered their ties to us. Silverado was peaceful for the few weeks that he convalesced after being hit by a car he'd been chasing. Weeks after the accident, Silver looked so forlorn that I knelt beside him, placing my face next to his. He threw up on me.

But my elementary-age sons loved him. So did my boyfriend, whom I married the next year despite him having purchased my four-legged nemesis.

As the years passed, my resentment toward Silver mellowed into grudging acceptance. My boys became teenagers, then young men. We moved to a house with a yard perfect for Silver to spend hours cavorting inside an electric fence. I gave birth to another son, who of course adored the gorgeous white dog whose energy, resistance to training and propensity for purposely yapping never waned.

But this year, after scampering good-naturedly past an age that my vet said many American Eskimos live to, Silverado, 14, began to sputter. He started limping intermittently, looking confused, soiling his sleeping quarters. A serious heart murmur would eventually kill him, the vet explained; severe arthritis was making movement difficult. The dog who couldn't stop moving stayed huddled in a corner.

Deep in the night, he barked us awake so he could relieve himself. On a recent morning at 3 a.m., I stood shivering in the dark. Silver peed as I pondered. The boys whose adoration ensured that an inappropriate pet became part of the family had grown up and gone. Somewhere they were sleeping, toasty and unaware.

Yet the woman who'd "hated" Silverado, who'd dreamed of freedom from his antics – and who wasn't a middle-of-the-night dog-walking type – couldn't bear to have him euthanized. It wasn't until Darrell, whose affection for Silverado never abated, arrived home from college, looked at him and said, "We should do it – he isn't happy," that I agreed.

With my husband leaving town, Darrell bravely offered to be present during the euthanasia. Phoning for an appointment, he froze when asked if he would stay in the room while Silverado was put to sleep. Realizing why he hesitated, I whispered, "Don't worry."

Silverado wouldn't die alone.

As the sad day neared, my son Skye, 10, was surprisingly stoic – until the day he blurted, "But what if heaven isn't real? Then I'll never see Silverado again." Nothing I said helped. Going online, I found Oldies But Goodies Cocker Spaniel Rescue of Northern Virginia, which provides care and homes to abandoned dogs and was the next day showing available cockers at a nearby PetSmart. Pet adoptions, the site explained, could take months. But the idea of seeing the dogs whose pictures we'd perused made Skye smile. We checked it out.

First to catch our eye: "Woofer," a tar-black 2-year-old cocker whose tail constantly wagged and who – bummer – was in the process of being adopted. We also were drawn to calm, chubby Penny and to Milly, an elegant blonde whose bearing reminded me of an aging movie star's. By the time we left, Skye and I both felt better.

Until Saturday. At noon, Darrell and I sat in a room at Kindness Animal Hospital in Wheaton, staring mutely at each other. In the next room, veterinarian Winnie Neunzig was placing a tiny catheter on Silverado's front right leg to ease the injection of a powerful barbiturate solution. Then she left him alone with us to say goodbye.

Darrell held Silver, rubbed his head, thanked him for being such a good friend. Then he rushed to the car, his tough-young-black-man cover forever blown.

Lifting Silverado onto the metal table where he'd for years received checkups, I took his face in both hands. Cooing "it's okay," Dr. Neunzig injected him. Silverado's black-marble eyes fastened onto mine; quite unexpectedly, I whispered, "I love you. I love you. I love you," until they closed.

With Neunzig patting my shoulder, I sobbed, lost in the puzzle that is love. Sometimes it's a warm wave that we gladly give ourselves over to. And sometimes it's a sneak-thief that corrals our hearts, seeping into our unconscious even as we're cursing its object.

Eight hours after Silver left us, a knock sent Skye to the door. Outside stood his surprise Christmas present. A dog whose would-be adopter, I'd learned the previous day, owned a cat that hissed at the notion of sharing its home with a curious cocker.

"Woofer!" Skye yelled.

It was meant to be. Our last gift to Silver, a bowl, had "WOOF" inscribed in the base.

A self-possessed charmer, Woofer loves being brushed, does his business outdoors, and at 3 a.m. is fast asleep in a delighted 10-year-old's bedroom. He's perfect.

Maybe some day I'll love him as much as Silverado.

Tom Tiede has been a syndicated columnist and newspaper publisher. His current blog is WhitherEudamonia.com. This column appeared during the Vietnam War.

The Grunt In The Grass – What A Man He Is

SAIGON – The average age of the combat GI in Vietnam is 18 and one-half.

But what a man he is.

A tousled-haired, tight-muscle fellow who, under normal circumstances, would be considered by society as half-grown, half-boy, not yet dry behind the ears, a pain in the unemployment chart. But now in boots and uniform, he is the beardless hope of free man.

He is, for the most part unmarried. He is likewise without material possessions, save for the old car at home and the transistor radio here in country.

He listens to rock and roll, and 105 howitzers.

He left high school, one way or the other, within the last year, received unimpressive grades, played a little football – and had a dolly who broke up with him when he went overseas, or swears she is still faithful, or has for whatever reasons stopped writing.

He has taken to beer because it is cold and because it is the thing to do. He smokes because he gets free sticks in his C-ration package, and it is also the thing to do. He is a Private First Class, a one-year veteran with one more to go. His eyes are clear but his future is not.

At home, he never cared for grunt labor. He preferred cruising the town to cutting the grass, sitting at the fast food joint rather than standing on the job. But he's lost 10 or more pounds now, working and fighting, dawn to dark. Big Macs are a memory.

He has trouble spelling, and letters home are a painful process. But he can break down a rifle in 30 seconds and put it back together in 29. He can describe the nomenclature of a fragmentation grenade, explain the operation of an M60 machine gun, and use where necessary.

He can also dig foxholes, apply first aid and march until he is told to stop.

He is obedient now. He follows orders. Yet he is not broken.

He has seen more suffering than he should have in his short life. He has seen men fall, or blown away, and he has walked in the blood for which he is partly responsible.

He has wept in private and in public, and been not ashamed either place.

And he's become oddly domestic. He has two pairs of fatigues, washes one and wears the other. He sometimes forgets to brush his teeth, but does not fail to clean his weapon. He keeps his socks dry, and his canteen wet. He is able as well to repair his injuries, mental or material.

He will share his water if you thirst, break his rations in half if you hunger, split his ammunition if you are battling for your survival.

He does the labor of two civilians, and draws half the pay. He has learned to use his hands as weapons, his weapons as hands and, whichever, he can save or take a life.

Eighteen and one-half.

What a man he is.

An Interview With The First Robin

The first robin of spring has appeared at the writer's free farm in central Virginia. He (or she) is a handsome bird who, nonetheless, will not provide his (or her) age or other personal information. This is the writer's interview with what is a feathered friend with an attitude.

The Writer: Where have you been all winter?

The Robin: That's the first question? You hit me up for a talk-talk, and you start with an inquisition. What kind of interview is this?

TW: Sorry.

TR: I mean, give me a break. I should be eating breakfast.

TW: Well, speaking of that, how are the worms?

TR: So-so, only so-so. Virginia worms taste like crickets.

TW: Crickets?

TR: You have to go to New Jersey to get great worms. The prob there is the air. Great worms, bad air. Plus, it's close to New York. New York has bad worms and bad air.

TW: I used to live in New Jersey.

TR: Is this interview about you or me?

TW: Sorry, again.

TR: As I was saying, bad air. The air in New Jersey puckers the beak.

TW: That's terrible.

TR: Except for crows. They get a bye. Now there's a rub.

TW: You don't like crows.

TR: They have no class. Caw, caw. They're not big on melody.

TW: So, I know you protect your privacy but are you married or anything?

TR: I was married. My spouse flew off to New Jersey to live with a sparrow.

TW: I thought birds of a feather flocked together.

TR: That was before Avian Liberation. Discrimination is out.

TW: I didn't know.

TR: It's called "birderhood."

TW: I see.

TR: Except hawks. Hawks do not subscribe to birderhood.

TW: What do they subscribe to?

TR: Kicking butts. Woo.

TW: OK. Getting back to worms, how do you find them?

TR: They are in the ground, pal.

TW: I mean, can you hear them crawling?

TR: You seem to have a thing about worms.

TW: I just…

TR: I thought you people only eat hamburgers.

TW: I…

TR: Most of you *look* like you only eat hamburgers.

TW: Right. Forget worms. It's spring. What are your plans?

TR: First, find a new mate. I have my eye on a woodpecker.

TW: And then?

TR: Fly high and poop on sidewalks. What else?

TW: I appreciate the interview, Mr. Robin. Thank you.
TR: Will it be on Google News?
TW: No, it will be on my site, Whither Eudaimonia.
TR: For this I missed breakfast?

Syndicated columnist Laverne Bardy is the author of "How the (Bleep) Did I Get This Old?" This column appeared June 13, 2012.

Buy Tan Towels And You, Too, Can Look Like A Zebra

I was channel-surfing and landed on the Home Shopping Network. I had assumed that people who buy from HSN were housebound, lonely or certifiable. Why else would anyone purchase items they can't first touch, smell, taste or try on?

Two women – each with perfect hair, Chiclet smiles and saccharin voices – were promoting stretch jeans. They waved their hands *a la* Vanna White, and described the color, texture, pockets, stitching and thrill of being able to remove them at the end of the day, and not find a red ring around their waist.

Red ring? How was it that I'd never had one of those? I felt cheated.

I never knew so much detail could be ascribed to a pair of pants, other than they come with a waistband, zipper and two openings for legs, which I don't recall them mentioning at all.

Callers phoned in, swooned and agreed that since they had been wearing those jeans they, too, were without red waistband rings. It became my mission to find someone with a red waistband ring and make him or her show me what I'd been missing.

Celia, from Atlanta, called and admitted to already having seven pairs of those incredible jeans, but decided to make it a nice round number by ordering five more.

"They're absolutely wonderful," she oozed. "I wear them for just about everything – digging in the garden, working in the office and, with the right accessories, I've even worn them to weddings and bar mitzvahs."

As they listened to Celia's review, the two saleswomen began salivating, barely able to contain their excitement. They reminded viewers not to wait another moment.

"Get to your phones or computers and order immediately. We've been advised that there are only 863 pairs of these unique jeans remaining, and you do not want to miss out on this stupendous offer."

I was prepared to switch channels when those two honey-tongued sweeties brought out a product that clutched at my heart: "Tan Towels" – self-tanning towelettes.

I live in New Jersey. I hadn't seen or felt sun on my body in more than five months. I look like I'd been dredged in flour. A few hours earlier, I remarked to my husband that it was time to head south because I had begun to blend in with the walls.

The camera zoomed in on the model's arms. One was pasty white, like mine. The other was a golden tan. She slid a moist Tan Towel over her untanned arm, and we were assured that within minutes she would look like she just returned from two weeks in Hawaii.

Before I could think it through, I picked up my credit card and phoned the number on the screen. I knew I had to do it immediately because there were only 6,003 Tan Towels left, and their phone lines were lighting up.

I made the fateful call and returned to the television, afraid I might miss something.

This time Margaret was on the phone She was extolling the magical wonders of Tan Towels, which she had purchased at an earlier date.

"I've been using them for several months now," she said. "They make me look and feel so good."

Sugar dripped from her lips as one of the beauties asked, "Margaret, would you mind telling our audience your age?"

"Not at all," she said. "I'm 84, and my boyfriend says I've never looked better."

The saleswomen could hardly catch their breath.

"Did you hear that?" one of them gasped. "Margaret is 84 and *still* cares about how she looks. How absolutely adorable!"

I froze in my tracks. Was there a cutoff date for caring how I look? I was 74. Margaret was 84 which meant, if I was lucky, I still had at least 10 years of caring ahead of me. I made a note to go to Google to find out how much time I had before I no longer gave a damn.

My Tan Towels arrived and I couldn't wait to start smearing them over my body. The HSN ladies assured me that my color would never turn orange or streak.

I hadn't realized that since the moisture was clear, there was no way of knowing whether was overlapping areas. Also, I couldn't reach my back.

I now look like a member of the animal kingdom –
leathery-brown knees and elbows and zebra-striped
body. Somehow I managed to totally miss my hairline so
I look like I'm wearing a white headband.

Does anyone know where I can buy a lightweight,
summery burka?

May 17, 2013

Some Unsupported Evidence

Are women better off without wearing bras? This topic
on night-time news, squeezed between Korea's nuclear
threats and the start of baseball season, has women
voicing some strong opinions. I, of course, am one of
those women. My first reaction is a resounding *"OMG!
Yes! Yes. Yes!"*

Jean Denis Rouillon, a professor at the Universite de
Franche-Comte in Besancon, France, conducted a study
in which he examined the breasts of 300 women, ages 18
through 35, over a 15-year period. His study concluded
that, "Bras provide no benefit to women and may
actually be harmful to breasts over time," and that
"Medically, physiologically and anatomically, the breast
does not benefit from being deprived of gravity."

I must step in here and applaud Professor Rouillon for
his courage in taking on such an arduous assignment.
This brave man single-handedly (OK, maybe he used
both hands) examined the breasts of 300 young women.
He worked, long, hard hours.

*(Hi, honey. Don't hold dinner for me. I'll be working
late…Yes, again.)*

Capucine Vercellotti, a 28-year-old woman who participated in the research, found that she breathed easier without the constraints of a bra. (*No kidding, Capucine. The only time I fully enjoy breathing is when I'm in the shower.*)

I knew from the first day I forced my arms behind my back and blindly attempted to find teensy metal hooks to fit into weensy metal eyes, that constraining and compressing my breasts was not in my best interest. Like caged animals, my girls have always cursed the inhuman individual who saw the need to restrain this part of my anatomy. All they ever wanted was to be free.

Maybe it made a modicum of sense to cover them in 1914 when 19-year-old Mary Phelps Jacob tied a couple of silk handkerchiefs together to conceal stiff whale bone stays that were visible through her sheer gown. But before long, the notion became a popular fashion statement as style-conscious women saw another way to start and follow a trend.

As luck would have it, someone, somewhere, decided those little silk handkerchiefs should do more than conceal whale bone. They might as well lift and separate also because – heaven forbid – time and gravity might eventually have their way, and they would lose the youthful perkiness God, and most men, believe they should have.

I love being a woman. I have never wanted to be a man but -- and I say this knowing full well I will be slammed by most of the female population – when it comes to fashion, sometimes women are morons. The greater majority will rush out and buy anything that fashion magazines dictate. But, if they had clearly thought this

bra issue through nearly 100 years ago, millions of
women would not have dents in their shoulders from
carrying around the weight of the world, and their
midriffs would not have to tolerate irritating fabric rub.
And for what? Just so bosoms wouldn't bounce.

Seriously?

I've harnessed my girls every day of my life since
eighth grade. When I told my mother that Jackie Young
had winked and asked me what I had in my gym-suit
pocket, she said it was time for me to wear a bra. And,
she promised, if I always wore it, my breasts would
never sag. Well, despite 62 painful years of doing what
Mother said, I have two words to describe what my girls
look like today: National Geographic.

When I was in fourth grade, I visited an eye doctor
who prescribed glasses.

"Don't wear them all the time," he said, "or you will
become too dependent on them."

I did what he suggested, and only wore them for seeing
the blackboard, reading and movies. Of course, the rest
of the time I bumped into walls and got into strangers'
cars. But the point is, I never found the need to rely on
them. And so it should be with bras.

Rouillon cautioned that women who have worn bras
for several decades would not benefit from taking their
bras off now.

Wanna bet? Stand back.

Patricia Bunin's "Senior Moments" columns have appeared in several papers of the Los Angeles Newspaper Group. She is a breast cancer survivor and creator of the breastbuddy.net support website. This column ran October 1, 2009.

I So Much Want Him
To Care What I Think

In case you missed it on *60 Minutes*, here's what CBS correspondent Andy Rooney thinks about older women:

"As I grow in age, I value women over 50 most of all. For example, a woman over 50 will never wake you in the middle of the night and ask, 'What are you thinking?' She doesn't care what you think."

My husband wants to know why I am not one of these women. I still want to know what he thinks – especially in the middle of the night. When I am usually not asleep. And he is, or would like to be, if I weren't keeping him awake asking important questions.

The darker and quieter it gets, the more active my mind becomes. Sometimes I have to really reach into the night's silence.

"Will you explain light years to me?" I asked George the other night, knowing it's hard for him to resist science-speak.

"You want me to explain that at 3 a.m.?"

"Why not?"

"What exactly do you need to know?"

"Why do they call them light years? Is that opposed to heavy years?"

"No, it's a measurement of distance."

"Then why not miles?"

"Because…are you just asking this just so I'll keep talking to you?"

"No, I've always wondered."

"And you have to know right now?"

"I'm not going to live forever."

I don't have the space to give you his full explanation, other than to tell you that it finally did put me to sleep.

But, in case you were wondering, a light year is 5 quadrillion, 878 trillion, 499 billion, 810 thousand miles. You never know when you will need a statistic like that, so keep it handy. It's not likely I'll be able to rattle if off again.

Stay tuned. I have a lot of sleepless nights. Who knows what I might learn next?

April 21, 2013

Ink In My Veins, Yeah, But Hands, Too

For George, it was frying pork chops and his Grandma Clara's peach cobbler. Ah, yes, the sweet smells of childhood.

For me, it was ink.

I got hooked at an early age. Lest you think I was sniffing it for some strange drug-related high, let me explain. Ink was one of my first smells of favor.

The Norfolk Virginian-Pilot was delivered to our house every morning. Long before I could read it, I was drawn to the smell, enticing and inviting. And what started with a friendship with the newspaper grew into a romance.

By age 10, I could be found on our front steps at 6 a.m., eagerly waiting for the paper to be delivered. OK, yes, I had a crush on Alan Frost, the cute guy who slung the paper from his bicycle basket. And, yes, I went out of my way to impress him by catching it. And, no, most of the time I did not. Catch it or impress him. But it didn't matter because once the paper came hurtling toward me I was lured by the link to ink. When it was finally in my hand, I forgot about him completely.

I loved the print that came off on my hands from turning the pages of the paper. It's more daring than dirty feel. The sense of secrets waiting to be shared. It's what I still love about newspapers. Folded anticipation.

There are new presents waiting to be unwrapped every day. Even though the paperboy has been replaced by someone driving a car who drops the paper in our driveway, I still eagerly await its arrival every morning.

Actually, on some days a cute guy, in the form of my husband, delivers the paper to me on a tray with morning tea. I smooth it out and take a bite of toast with my inky hand. As much a part of my morning meal as the jam on my toast, the paper is a sweet start to my day.

No, I don't take a bite out of it, nor should you, but do take a moment to smell the ink.

**Dennis McCann wrote for the Milwaukee Journal
and, later, the Milwaukee Journal Courier for almost
25 years. His books include "Badger Boneyards: The
Eternal Rest Of The Story." This column was written
in the 1990s.**

Digger, The Old Cemetery Man,
Is A Dying Breed

NORWAY, Mich. – This story comes from about six
feet over the Wisconsin-Michigan border, but no
artificial boundary should get in the way of a good
cemetery tale. Someone once told me when I got to this
area I should slip across the border and visit Digger.

Digger is really Ed Wenzel, but also called Billy. He
was 76 when we met in the early 1990s and might truly
be called the last of a dying breed – a small-town sexton
who knows where the bodies are buried because he
buried them.

When I called to say I was coming, I was struck by
Digger's distinctive Upper Peninsula accent, so I bought
a tape recorder that night and took it with me the next
day.

Digger was wearing a cap and work clothes, but with
no immediate need to arrange for another permanent
lodger, he had time to show me around the piney setting
where he worked.

I'd been told to ask Digger about the old days so I did.

"1937. April the first. 1937," he said. "When I walked
up here the first day, it was really like a son of a gun.
You had to walk four miles; there were no cars them
days. There was no building, nothing. Just a little old

dark shed down in a hole. They had a wheelbarrow, a shovel and a rake; that's all they had. Steel wheel, too.

"You had to dig everything by hand, and then wheel everything to the woods by wheelbarrow because there's half the grave left over. Anybody with common sense knows that…

"Like I said, you had no place to eat, no shed, 30 below you had to come out and dig. You had to shovel the snow by hand, no snow-blow, all with a scoop shovel. Then I started to plow with a truck without no door. That's how I froze my face.

"(I got) a dollar and a half a day, and then the other guys got a dollar and a quarter. I got a quarter more because I took the foreman's job. I did it all, take care of the books, the whole damn thing. And I never was a bookkeeper. I was a gravedigger and I told 'em that. Now I get, well, a guy shouldn't put salaries in there…

"We only get $325 here for digging a grave. They get six and eight hundred in Iron Mountain…See, we don't have no backhoe. We could have one, but to me it don't seem feasible. It's only sand, you know.

"We dig 'em all by hand. Couple of hours in the sand and we dig a hole, and one hour after we're done…you couldn't even tell where he was buried. We dig 'em all year 'round. I dug at 30 below. You gotta pound with a hammer and maul and dig 'em. When you're young you can go like heck. Like I said, it's sand…but like I said, it ain't easy.

"And I hate to say it, but if I hadn't never stayed here they wouldn't have the cemetery like it is. I don't want to brag about myself, but I know, because I keep this up like I keep my yard at home.

"But I'm only one man and I'm getting older. I can't cut the mustard like I used to. Because I fell off the roof five years ago and about killed myself.

"My wife rolled me over and I heard her long miles away saying, 'Eddy, your father's gone, I think. I think your father is gone, go call the ambulance. I think your poor, old father is dead.' But then I started to roll a bit. She said, 'Oh Lord amighty, he's starting to move.'

"A woman the other day said, 'I never thought you'd be back digging holes again, you were pretty well battered.' I broke my arm and my collarbone and my pelvis, but I got out of the damn bed and came back and dug again.

"You got to be a cemetery man. You got to be dedicated. You got to go with the weather. When there's snow, you know, or a goddarn rainstorm you got to be out there, you got to get that goddarn thing in the ground. If the man says the funeral is 10 o'clock Tuesday, it's 10 o'clock Tuesday. Even though you are dead, you are on time."

We sat for a while in the sexton's office where large historic photographs served as décor.

"Oh, yeah, all the miners from that top picture up there, I buried the whole damn bunch of them," Digger said. "Even the widows…My mother, my father, my brothers, I did. I dug my mother's on Sunday. I dug all my relations, too. It never bothered me. Yesterday I buried my classmate. When (someone) calls up and says so-and-so's dead, you kind of feel funny. You get used to it, like anything else.

"Years ago, I done all the digging, but now I get my son Eddy and them kids, they like that, see…

"But I know when I'm gone, the day I walk out of there, they're going to go mechanized, I know they are."

We drove through the cemetery where I met a host of dead people.

"The first grave I dug was right here," Billy would say, a man at peace with his accomplishments.

He is at home here, and like a good cemetery man he has planned ahead. His stone is in place, and he knows who will open the Earth to receive him.

"Eddy," he said. Like father, like son.

October 11, 2007

After The Multiple Murders, Stronger Still

Editor's note – The man who killed the six young people, Tyler James Peterson, was a deputy on the local sheriff's department. One of Peterson's victims at the post-homecoming party was his former girlfriend. Authorities believe an argument between the two led to the murders.

CRANDON, Wis. – On the very first day horrific headlines of multiple murders in his community spread around the world, Crandon Mayor Gary Bradley vowed to reporters that his city would heal. Crandon, he said, would pick itself up by the bootstraps, as it always has before.

"We are a strong community," he said. "We always have been."

Crandon has always had to be strong. Born in the rugged tall timber of Wisconsin's far north in the last

years of the 1800s, it has always been a low-frills town --
more rough-cut than polished, a place of woods and
water and recreation, but never a fancy Up North resort
destination.

Throughout its history, the town has been a place that
demanded hard work even as it did not always reward it
– a place where earning life's necessities was always a
more realistic dream than attaining life's luxuries.

It is a community settled by hardy pioneers as so many
places were, but not one that forgot that history the way
so many others did.

"The pioneers were all on a level, so far as money is
concerned," one account of the early days said. "They
were all poor, but independent."

Today, residents still shop at Pioneer Plaza, still read
the Pioneer Express weekly newspaper and eat at the
Log Cabin Café. Gentrification has never been an issue.

And it is a community that cannot be separated from
the rest of Forest County, of which it is the county seat,
or from the sprawling forest that gave rise to the name.
The whole county was born out of logging, not just
Crandon. Of Wisconsin's 72 county seats, Crandon is the
only one that features live deer in pens on the courthouse
square – four does in one and two bucks in the other, this
week sporting the impressive racks that bucks do as the
rut approaches.

But nobody was looking at the deer on Tuesday. A few
yards away, cameras from around the state and beyond
were clicking and whirring at the bullet-shattered
window of a Crandon squad car put on display for
reporters. It was the car in which one officer was shot at
while pursuing another officer gone wrong.

The gunman was Tyler James Peterson, who early on Sunday killed six young people – young people "about to enter the prime of their lives," Attorney General J.B. Van Hollen put it – and wounded another before dying himself, apparently by his own hand.

That's what Crandon has to be strong about now.

It is easy to overdo the big-city-bad, small-town-good thing. As Milwaukee was too long forced to serve as a punch line for Jeffrey Dahmer jokes, little Plainfield in central Wisconsin still suffers from its one degree of separation from its own most infamous son, Ed Gein. Bad and good and big and small can be mixed and matched.

"It's a great place to live," said Mike Monte on Tuesday night, sitting in the office of the Pioneer Express amid the clutter of a small-town newspaper and preparing to write something on perhaps the biggest single story of his life, although none of his 8,500 subscribers wanted to read much more about.

Monte initially wasn't going to answer any questions, citing the attorney general's plea on behalf of local residents that reporters stop asking and that residents and officials stop answering.

But he yielded when the subject was Crandon and not crime. A native son and longtime logger before he bought the Pioneer Express and began also writing about area history, Monte can attest to his mayor's suggestion that Crandon has often had to struggle to keep up.

The city, and newly created Forest County, boomed when the railroad finally arrived and mills built to harvest the forest's timbered riches. After the Page & Landeck mill opened in 1901, the city grew from 800 residents to more than 2,400. Monte wrote in his book, "Cut & Run: Logging Off the Big Woods," a tale of fortunes made while the woods were being cut and lives left adrift when they were gone.

After logging, the lumber companies sold the "cutover" land to settlers who dreamed of living the good farm life. Instead, the land was so rocky and stump-riddled it demanded back-breaking work to clear enough land even to plant. The University of Wisconsin ran a Land Clearing Special train to the cutover to teach settlers the safe way of dynamiting stumps so they would have hands and fingers enough to farm if they ever did clear their acres.

And that was before the Great Depression hit.

"The Depression," Monte said, "lasted here longer than elsewhere." Just as the hard times had begun there years before they hit Wall Street in 1929.

One enterprise that helped sustain some in the area was moonshining. Hundreds of Crandon's settlers had come from Kentucky, where Page & Landeck had closed another mill, and they brought with them both Appalachian accents and a talent for making whisky. It was, Monte said, "One of the things that kept people going." Crandon still holds an annual Kentucky Day celebration.

Then came World War II, which took so many men away, and the 1950s, when still more left for jobs in cities like Milwaukee and the Fox Valley. Some would come back on weekends and show off their check stubs in a "see-how-much-I-make" way intended to impress those who had stayed behind.

When he returned from college to go into the woods as a logger in 1971, Monte said, he was one of only a few headed that way. Most others who wanted work were going elsewhere, including to Vietnam.

Today Crandon might offer more to high school graduates than in earlier years, he said. Tourism creates some jobs. Rhinelander's opportunities are 25 miles away. And, of course, there is still logging, although more high-tech now than when it created lots of jobs.

Still, he said, "We get a bad reputation sometimes. Let's face it, this isn't a place where you find many bachelor degrees." Modern logging requires smarts, skills and hard work, he said, "but doesn't get you much respect statewide."

Crandon isn't asking for respect now, although respecting its privacy would be nice and allowing it to grieve and get on would be better. In his office Tuesday evening, Monte was considering what to write, not wanting to further hurt raw feelings in his readership.

"I'm not going to be talking about the gory details. I'm going to be talking about the healing," he said. "We'll recover from this as a community."

For now, it just has to be strong.

John Blankenship writes for the Register-Herald in Beckley, W. Va. This column appeared Feb. 7, 2014.

No Pictures, Please, With My Obit

Dying is no laughing matter. But I can't help wondering what I should include in my obituary; the humor and the care required to tell my final story in print.

An editor asked me recently if I had any personal history on file in the library, which we call the morgue. "That way, we don't have to go digging if something should happen," she explained.

Does she know something I don't?

In a small but growing number of newspapers, obituaries are no longer just dull pieces written by green reporters or tired old-timers who seem to be copying from a funeral register.

Now, obituaries are among the best-written, most informative stories in newspapers. More importantly, they now seek to give a true picture of the dead person's life, touching on the bad as well as the good.

Some high-quality obituary writers regularly interview aging notables and prepare their eulogies in advance. Some even set these tributes in type, but others don't. A few editors apparently consider it bad luck for the person being probed on such matters.

If I were being queried for my obituary notice, I think I would be flattered. After all, we're all going to die, so why not welcome the opportunity to chat about our life's experiences while we're still around?

I would want to place some value on it and point out what I think is essential, or what I want to be remembered for. Besides, some of us like to see our names in print, but that doesn't mean we sit around waiting to die.

Unfortunately, when most people get close to death's dark foyer, they've pretty much had it with life. Their outlook is, "I won't be able to read it when it runs, and I'm not interested in reading it now."

I think some of those suffering souls just want to get life over with. They would say, "Just give me oblivion; I've had enough…" And they would prefer their obit to be short and sweet, or at least to the point.

Some newspapers have such large circulations that they run obits on only a small percentage of the people who die in their cities. If a laborer dies at 100, or jumps off the top of a tower, they're interested.

But if a guy succumbs to cirrhosis of the liver, or some other mundane medical ailment, they're usually not as keen for an opus on his passing.

Some smaller papers try to run obituaries on everyone who passes away in their circulation area, but these honors are often just token attempts that don't even tell the cause of death.

Cancer kills one of six Americans. But small papers often refer to the disease only as a "lingering illness," or with some other euphemism, primarily because relatives don't like to disclose that a person died of cancer.

While some relatives don't want to list the cause of death, others are leery of listing the address of the deceased.

There's good reason for that. Obits and paid death notices are among the best-read parts of a paper, and the readers include burglars who like to pay their respects by visiting the home of the dead person during the funeral. Likewise, real estate agents also are avid readers of obituaries, hoping to find a widow who wants to sell her home.

Ernest Hemingway lived to see his obituary printed. He was seriously injured in two plane crashes in Africa in 1953 and was twice reported dead. Several newspapers ran their praises of the American author before the news that he hadn't yet departed reached them.

"Most of the obituaries I could never have written nearly as well myself," Hemingway reportedly joked.

Some people actually have the chance to write their own obit. An aging friend of mine did just that before he passed away a few years ago. I was asked to add a flourish to the final commentary, which I was honored to do. But it was a sad thing.

I wonder if my obit will make Page One. I doubt it, but I hope it carries my byline.

It will probably begin with something like this: "I died late yesterday afternoon on my veranda while smoking a Havana cigar."

No pictures, please.

Please, Officer, Would You Mind Not Pointing Your Gun At Me?

I've been working for newspapers for much of my life. Most of my career has been spent with Beckley Newspapers, a publication I joined nearly 50 years ago.

Before that, I labored for a couple of small-town dailies and weeklies. I go back to a time when typesetters worked in hot lead and wore square caps of folded newspaper to keep the ink out of their hair. It was an era when stories were written on manual typewriters, typed on reams of copy paper, edited with pencils and cobbled together with foul-smelling glue.

The folks who wrote and edited the news were a ribald, coarse and bawdy bunch. They were lewd, funny and generally an insensitive lot. A number of reporters, especially those on the cop beat, carried small-caliber handguns in their coat pockets, and some of the boozy editorial bosses kept bottles of cheap whisky in their desk drawers.

If publishes objected, we never heard about it. Besides, a few old-timers of the trade owed the family-owned business so much borrowed money that the owners kept them on in hopes of eventually recovering some of the debt.

All in all, it made for a rousing place to work.

The newsrooms of the past featured a kind of dramatic spirit that's mostly missing from today's information centers with their confined cubicles, mute compartments and stern manner that discourage the facetious and silly side of human nature.

One of the first assignments I got as a young reporter was to photograph a man who had been severely beaten up and robbed at a local junkyard. When the film was developed and the pictures printed, the images failed to disclose any of the rips and gouges to the victim's scalp and forehead. So my editor sent me out to do the job again.

"You idiot," he snarled. "Either get a shot of the man's head wounds or don't come back! You got that?"

My next photo effort ran on the front page. It was a close-up of the victim pointing to his skull injuries that required a great deal of needlework to mend.

Soon after that, I landed a job on the police beat, but I was fearful of going near the police station. Several of the cops had threatened to shoot me on sight if they caught me on the premises.

In one of my stories, I had noted that a squad car had run over a woman fleeing the scene of a traffic stop. She suffered third-degree burns on her legs from the cruiser's exhaust pipes and I deemed the incident newsworthy.

The investigating officers didn't agree. After the story ran, the reaction I got from the local police bureau was, "We don't need any reporters around here! You got that?"

Back in those days, some cops would mirthfully pull their weapons out and point them at young reporters in an effort to intimidate them. It was some kind of initiation custom, I suppose. Anyway, I complained to the chief of police who took a dim view of the practice, but said it wasn't up to him to tell his patrolmen when to draw their weapons or where to point them.

"I try not to interfere with the force doing its job," he said cheerfully.

Eventually, I managed to win over the city police department with my fair and accurate reporting style, and often was invited to go out on drug and gambling busts in the city.

It was a romantic world that lured me in my youth and one that still has a hold on me today – although newspapers have changed greatly since those early days of my career.

Computers have replaced the typewriters and typesetting is a lost art. The printers' hats, the copy paper and the glue pots are long gone and editors and policemen, in particular, seem more civilized than their counterparts of the past.

Still, the most important qualities of a newspaper remain the same: Record the events of the day, chronicle the issues, entertain, inform and provide fodder for discussion and debate. It's the town crier, the mirror and sometimes the conscience of the community.

I have worked with many talented editors and publishers and am grateful for their faith and their care. I look forward to a few more years in a profession that is often described as one of the most interesting jobs on Earth.

John Schneider wrote a column for the Lansing, Mich., State Journal from 1988 until 2012. He pens a monthly column for "Bridge," an online magazine. His play, "Voice Mail," takes place in a newsroom.

A Candle To Help
Handle The Darkness

Words you don't ever want to hear:

"Have you ever considered…would you consider… the 'Gift of Life', regarding your daughter?"

A bubble of rage and fear rises from deep inside your chest and nearly chokes you. You think: "Where's OUR gift? Where's HER life? What stranger is going to come along and give US what we need?"

It's not the logistics that repulse you, because you know that the human corpse, reclining on a gurney somewhere in the hospital, is no longer your daughter. The "Gift of Life" folks are correct in their silent implication that what's left is merely a collection of organs and tissues that might be of use in prolonging – or improving – life elsewhere. If we hurry.

It is the black, bottomless, unfathomable finality implied by the question – that's what squeezes the breath out of you when the hospital social worker, or whatever she is, gently tosses it up from behind her desk and it falls upon you like a steel beam.

But you hear your wife saying, "Yes. Of course. Whatever would be helpful…," almost as though she had considered it and thought it through to the end. Almost as though she had decided it was the right thing to do, despite her personal pain, and assumed that you, too, would leap at the chance to pull something good from this disaster.

And, in your wife's lack of hesitation – her calm certainty – you find the breath to concur with her decision. You don't say, "We need a minute to discuss this," or, "Maybe we should think about this a little more." The words leap forth, seemingly under their own power.

"Yes. Absolutely."

At the time of that decision, before you've begun to realize that healing is even a possibility, the commitment feels merely like a rational and decent thing to do. You can't think of any reason NOT to do it.

So, you sign the necessary papers.

Only later does it become one of the things that sustains you. Only further down the road, when you sense that there is a path out of the tunnel, after all, do you conjure up that moment in that tiny room in the hospital, when you said "yes," and hold that moment in front of you, like a candle. It becomes one of the many candles you'll carry against the darkness.

In the following weeks, the letters arrive:

- From the Midwest Eye Banks and Transplantation Center: "Because of your compassion, a young woman from Oregon, Ohio, and a young man from Detroit are able to see again, following corneal transplantation. We hope there is some comfort in knowing that you have created a memorial for your daughter, who lives in the minds and hearts of those whose lives are forever changed."

- From "Gift of Life": "Jessica…contributed bone, heart valves and other tissues. The bone will be used in the treatment of deformities of the spine…The heart valves will benefit persons who suffer anomalies of the heart…The other tissues will help people who require reconstructive surgery, because of trauma or illness…I would like to express our gratitude for your willingness to assist desperately ill people you have never met."

So, groping and lurching, you shuffle forward, steadying yourself by whatever means are available, guided by the light.

Editor's note – Jessica suffered a seizure and drowned in Lake Huron on August 17, 2002.

Tigers Opener Takes On Rangers, Mom's Dictum

DETROIT (AP) – The Detroit Tigers are taking heat from Roman Catholics who criticize the scheduling of the club's home opener during holy hours on Good Friday. Traditional Christian belief says Jesus hung on the cross from noon to 3 p.m. on Good Friday.

Picture this: You're 11 years old, and it's the first day of your 10-day Easter break. It's April, and the air is thick with the first muddy whiff of spring.

You're a bud, bursting with pent-up energy. You're a crocus, eager to flex your vitality in the sun.

You're a wild colt released from your pen into the inviting arms of an endless pasture.

You and your pals, stripped down to T-shirts, are prancing, and bucking, kicking up your heels. You're organizing baseball games, flying kites, building forts, wallowing in the mud.

But it's Good Friday. Noon is approaching. Before you left the house that morning, your Irish-Catholic mother reminded you of your holy obligation. She laid out your options, one more odious than the other.

Ideally, you would shed your smelly tennis shoes, comb your hair and hike the mile to St. Thomas Aquinas Parish to endure the Stations of the Cross – a few of them anyway. But since that would be like volunteering to spend an extra day in civics class, you'll go with Option 2: house arrest.

So, at noon – just as the neighborhood action is really heating up – you're obligated to slouch home to your tuna fish sandwich and three hours of incarceration.

"Where are you going?" your Protestant chums ask as you slink away. No point in trying to explain it. "To prison," you say.

From noon to 3 p.m. there is no TV, no fighting, rowdy play or torturing your siblings – at least not blatantly – which, your mother points out, would run contrary to the spirit of religious reflection.

You can read, but not comic books. No "Mad" magazines either.

"But what can I do?" goes your anguished cry.

"Count your blessings – and think about what you can do to become a better person," your mother replies.

So, you sit, or you lie, or you pace the floor, as the voices of your frolicking friends penetrate even the storm windows of your bedroom. That three hours is an immovable block, a granite cliff yielding imperceptibly, over eons, to the ocean's wave.

You do a little math…180 minutes…10,800 seconds.

The Associated Press story continued:

"All 30 American and National League teams play April 10, but the Tigers 1:05 game against the Texas Rangers is the only one during holy hours. The Rev. Ed Vilkauskas of downtown Detroit's St. Mary's Catholic Church tells the Detroit Free Press the game will keep people away from services."

Maybe, when you brought your opening day tickets you didn't realize it would be played on Good Friday.

Maybe, as the Star-Spangled Banner spreads out over the

field like a pad of butter on a hot skillet, you'll think of what your mother would say.

But only in a smiling sort of way. You're not going home. It's springtime. You've put in a good Lent. It's time for baseball.

Josh Freed is a newspaper columnist for the Montreal Gazette in Canada. His latest book is titled "He Who Laughs, Lasts." He also produces documentary films. This column appeared September 10, 2011.

A Plague Of Passwords

To read this column, please answer the following security questions:

What was your second grade teacher's first pet's name?

What is your favorite color?

What is my favorite color?

I was travelling recently and dropped in at an Internet café. But when I tried to get my email, I was struck by a terrifying modern disease: password amnesia. I couldn't recall which password I used for my Hotmail. Was it joshf or jfreed? Or freedjosh?

No, that was my Borders Book Club password. Or was it my barbershop gold card code?

At home, my computer automatically stores all my passwords, but while travelling, I have to remember them – and they're blurred into a jumble after two weeks away. Like a hacker trying to break into someone's computer, I took a few educated guesses.

I tried my street name, my son's name and my wife's birthday. I tried the top-secret code I have for banking – but what the heck did I change that to the last time I lost my card? My grandmother's maiden name, backwards? Or my height in centimeters followed by my age when I took piano lessons?

The fact is we all suffer from occasional password amnesia – because we have too many passwords. We used to need a secret password or number for serious security matters like credit cards, Swiss bank accounts and automatic garage openers. But now everyone insists we have one, in a plague of passwords.

I need passwords for my Hotmail and Gmail, bank cards and phone cards, phone plans and Airmile plans. I have passwords for Apple, Amazon, eBay, iTunes, Ticketmaster and my Stairmaster.

Just to hear my own phone messages in my own house I must punch in *98 and then my security password. Who am I protecting myself against? Is there a wave of burglars breaking into houses and ransacking voice mail boxes?

"Hey, Lefty, forget the diamonds! They've got phone messages!"

Most people have one high-security password for important stuff and one low-security password they can easily recall – usually their street name or their hamster's name. But many sites have strict rules and reject your password if it doesn't have 10 letters and include a number, a capital letter and an umlaut.

So you have to modify your password slightly. Then when you log in you can't remember which version to use: josh1, josh9 or josh with an umlaut?

Type your password incorrectly three times and you'll get your account suspended and have to talk to Password Control as they try to "verify your identity." They'll ask you security questions about your first middle school, your second husband and your last mistress. Then they'll

make you "reset" your password with a new one – and
suddenly, you've got something else to forget.

*We interrupt this column for a security check. An
unauthorized user may be on this page trying to read this
story and your mind, in an attempt to steal your
password to knittingworld.com. Please answer the
following security questions:*

What was the name of your neighbor's hamster?
What do these letters say: Zcbgx5 &^$# -- in Greek?
What is your bank PIN number?

Another hoop we must now jump through is
deciphering weird distorted letters onscreen that we must
retype correctly. For instance, if you want to email
someone a curry recipe from gourmetrecipes.com, you
must first identify blurry letters that seem to spell
"ypoletka Brezhnev."

It's a bit like an eye doctor chart but harder to read, so
I usually fail and must try another set of letters that looks
like "grfzuhs cereal" – and I fail again and decide I don't
want to email that recipe anyway.

I'd told these eye exams are to prove we are humans,
not computers that are programmed to constantly scan
the net trying to steal everyone's identity. Apparently,
machines can't read these distorted letters, so by
deciphering them we prove we are people. So why do I
feel like I'm being turned into a machine instead?

Why do we need so much security anyway? Are we a
nation of secret agents? The average person now has
more secret passwords than the Allied Supreme
Commander did during World War II.

Is this really necessary? Are we living in a dangerous
electronic world where we're constantly at risk of having

our identity robbed if we don't change our Pizza World password every 90 days?

Or are we just victims of a paranoid, overzealous security system that's developed a life of its own by wasting ours? Whatever the answer, I suspect it will only get worse. Soon our microwaves, toasters and blenders will all require passwords, too. After we have been verified by Visa, we will be reverified by "Verified by Verified by Visa."

It won't be long before computers learn to read those distorted letters, too – and we'll need new and more profound ways to prove we're human. My new personalized stove will lock me out and demand a password based on recipes only I could know.

"Please answer this question: What temperature do you use to bake your mother's famed lasagna casserole?"

Frankly, I dream of a day when I have one universal code tattooed on my ear, or my rear. Sure, someone may break into all my systems and listen to my phone calls, then read my junk mail – but I don't really mind, as long as they answer it all, too.

I'm tired of living like a secret agent, since I don't really have that many secrets. Except for my Hotmail password – whatever it is.

September 10, 2005

Who Took The Chit Out Of Chat?

I took an airport cab recently where the driver and I chatted nonstop the entire ride – only we weren't talking to each other. He was yakking on his cellphone and I was on mine, each in our own private worlds.

I love talking to cabbies, armchair experts on everything from local news and traffic to politics in their distant native lands. But more and more of them now pull out their hands-free phone the second I sit down and treat me like a package in the back seat.

Ask a question and they'll say, "Excuse me, sir, but I am talking to my mother in Cairo."

Since they're ignoring me, I ignore them. It's a chance to get some work done – but one less chance to enjoy the company of strangers.

Cabs are just one of many places where random conversations with strangers are getting hard to find. We used to talk to the butcher, the baker and candlestick-maker – but most of them have been replaced by big-box stores where customer relations matter more than human relations.

The clerks at big-box stores often ask: "Did you find everything you were looking for, sir?" But they don't really want you to say anything but, "Yes, I did, thanks," even if you didn't. Trying to make conversation with them is practically rude.

I tried to chat with a supermarket cashier recently and she looked at me like she was going to call for security. "Attention! Attention! Weird bald guy at Aisle 3 who wants to TALK."

I can still chit-chat at my local cheese shop, newsstand, or stationery store, but the neighborhood gas guy who checked my oil and talked to me about the weather is long gone. He's been replaced by a self-service place with a cashier who's way too busy selling lottery tickets to converse.

In recent years, bank machines have ended our chats with tellers, while the phone operator has long vanished, replaced by PRESS 1 machines. It's the same when we phone offices, where I used to get personal secretaries I'd gradually get to know.

But now I get a voice machine instead – or at best the voice mail of a secretary. An hour later they return my call and leave a message and later I call and leave them one – and by the time we're through messaging we've said what we needed and don't end up talking.

Worst are airplanes where no one talks to their seatmates anymore – we're all too busy watching our little TVs. Your seatmate won't hear you even if you shout, "The plane's on fire!" because we're all wearing earphones.

The conversational blackout even extends to friends and family. For much of my life, I called my pals at home and never knew who'd pick up the phone. I might end up talking to their spouse, or their kids, or their cleaning woman – in unexpected chats.

But the last couple of years I barely remember my friends' home numbers – I just call their cellphones, which they answer immediately. As a result, I never have random chats with whoever else answers – because no one else does.

The irony is we've never heard more about "chat." There are chat rooms, chat lines and chat shows – but real chat is disappearing. We walk in crowds of people, all talking on our cellphones, living in our own private cells. We listen to iPods, each with our own soundtrack.

We send email invitations instead of making phone calls because fewer words are lost in random chatter. But something else is lost as isolation replaces conversation.

Taxis are even more isolating now that most cabs have passenger TVs so you end up watching your own screen in back while the driver chats privately up front. Maybe we should develop robot taxis that are more chatty, to take over this human task.

- *Welcome to Robo-Cab. Please state your destination.*
- *Downtown, please.*
- *Thank you. Robo-Cab now proceeding to destination. Would you prefer my Silent Driver function or my Chatty Driver one? I can converse on many subjects.*
- *Press 1 to hear me complain about construction hassles on the Interstate thru-way.*
- *Press 2 to discuss politics in my native land. I was built in China.*
- *Press 3 for a rant on cheap taxi fares and how many hours I put in driving.*

Until then, what must you do to put the chit back in chat? Next time you're in the supermarket, put down your cellphone and talk to your aisle-mate. When you go to the dentist, ask the assistant how her teeth are. Or try discussing the news with the guy at your newsstand.

Chat up a stranger today – and help make society more social.

Stu Bykofsky has been a columnist on the Philadelphia Daily News since 1987. Prior to penning the column, he was a theater critic. This column appeared September 28, 1994.

Dog's Cruel Death
At Hands Of Animals

Duke didn't deserve to die. Not like he did.

Duke was unusual, a Dalmatian with chocolate markings, a loyal family pet for 6 ½ years. The storied fireman's friend, Dalmatians are prized for their looks, their pep, their devotion.

Duke didn't deserve to be tortured, maimed and murdered for the sport of brutes who fall a mile short of "human."

Three men have been accused – Roy A. Elliott and Jason Tapper, both 21, and Jan W. Pyatt, Jr., 23. If what is said about them is true, they are a nightmare.

Since they have not had their preliminary hearing – more about that in a minute – justice cloaks them in the presumption of innocence.

But I'm not a judge. I'm just a guy who has looked at the file and a court document.

Here are the facts so far:

Duke's owners, Mary and Patrick Callahan, were moving from the large Huntingdon Valley home in which they raised seven kids to a condo that doesn't permit pets. At a high-school graduation/going-away party at their home for youngest daughter Katie, 18, they met some of Katie's friends, one of whom had brought Pyatt and Tapper.

They told the Callahans they lived on 10 acres, had other animals and would give Duke a good home. Even better, their place was near the Callahans' new condo, so Mary, 56, would be able to visit her Duke often. In fact, before letting Pyatt and Tapper take Duke, Mary said she'd visit the very next day to make sure her dog was getting along all right.

Duke really was her dog, a Christmas gift she received from the kids when Duke was an 8-week-old puppy. As Duke grew to a fit and healthy 55 pounds under her care, Mary and Duke developed a daily love ritual.

Each day when Mary came home from work, "He would greet me and I would say, 'Oh, Duke, oh Duke, let's have some lovey time.' '' Duke would leap on the couch, bury his head between the pillows while Mary scratched and tickled him. Duke would nuzzle Mary and make little sounds of delight. "It was our Dukey time, our lovey time," said Mary.

The Callahans wanted to find him a good home because Duke was a good dog – loyal, protective of the family and trusting. The Callahans were trusting, too, for which Mary now is heart-sick.

She gave Duke to Pyatt and Tapper, but that night Mary was told by one of Katie's friends that Duke supposedly jumped out of the car on the way to his new home in Warrington and was loose in Hatboro. Upon hearing this, the Callahans searched for Duke in their van, put up posters and knocked on doors.

Their search was in vain, because they were searching for something that was not lost.

I believe Duke wasn't really lost because a week after his disappearance, his mutilated remains were found. Not in Hatboro, but in a field behind Pyatt's home.

There is also a witness who related that on the same day the Callahans were putting Duke into what they believed were kind hands, Duke's mouth was taped shut, he was tied to a tree, and Pyatt's pit bull was turned loose on the defenseless family pet. The savage brute fixed it so the terrified Dalmatian could neither fight nor run.

Duke's torment didn't end with the pit bull (now in SPCA custody). After the attack, according to a veterinarian's examination of Duke's remains, his tail was cut off, his belly was cut open, his throat was slit, his skull was crushed. He was discarded like so much trash.

Duke didn't deserve to die. Not like that.

"I will never forgive myself for giving him to those bastards," says a guilt-stricken Mary. She's barely able to handle the grief of thinking that her Duke suffered and died in vain, and now makes it her mission to warn people never to surrender beloved pets to anyone they're not sure of.

I called lawyers for the accused, asking for an interview. No dice.

I had just a couple of questions I wanted to ask, if the charges have any truth in them at all:

How did you get so low? How can you bear to live with yourself?

You don't have to be a dog lover to hate this crime. You don't have to be a dog lover to believe that if these three are guilty and get off with a slap on the wrist, they may graduate to bigger and better things.

If guilty, what they need are heavy fines and stiff jail sentences for what Bucks County SPCA director Anne Irwin calls "the most vicious incident of deliberate cruelty we've ever prosecuted" in her 23 years with the SPCA. If guilty, they also desperately need psychiatric counseling.

The preliminary hearing is scheduled for Oct. 21 at 11:30 a.m. in Magisterial Courthouse in Warrington. The Callahans will be at the hearing, and so will I. My wife, and my dog, will stand outside the courthouse as silent witnesses for Duke.

You can join us there, alone or with your pet.

Duke didn't deserve to die. Not like that.

Editor's note – The three men were convicted of felony animal fighting and sentenced to serve at least three and one-half years in prison.

November 15, 2004

Dapper Tom Always Makes Us Proud

The last time I saw Tom Foglietta was a year ago at the funeral of his dear friend from South Philly, cardiologist Ron Pennock.

Tom was dapper as always, but very sad, because Pennock had been a close friend and frequent traveling companion. During the few years that Tommy was ambassador to Italy, Pennock logged a lot of time at

126

Villa Taverna, the mansion-like ambassador's residence in Rome.

I spent a few days at Villa Taverna in 1998, doing a story on the ambassador. Other of Foglietta's friends did the same, but without the "work" excuse.

Even at 75, Tommy had John Kerry hair – a full, rich, youthful headful that had turned slate-gray but not white.

During my 1998 visit with him, I was going to report the 69-year-old ambassador was squiring around an Italian TV personality – a glamorous brunette – who was about half his age.

For only the second time, Tommy asked me not to mention something in a column – this time his age.

I agreed. I wasn't sure if he didn't want his age used because the woman didn't know, or because he thought it was undiplomatically age-inappropriate.

One other thing he asked me not to do. When writing about him as a politician, as a footloose bachelor, as a congressman, I would occasionally refer to him as Fog, or the Fog.

After he became ambassador, he asked me to drop the Fog moniker because he felt it seemed disrespectful to the high office.

I put that Fog nickname to sleep.

I know he loved being ambassador. He loved having a police escort through Roman traffic, he loved the lavish dinners at Taverna and in restaurants (how he kept slim, I'll never know). I know he loved skiing in the Alps, he loved the access the American ambassador got to balls and parties, and he loved being the face of America to the country that had produced his parents.

The Italians loved him, too. I saw how he was cheered wherever he went. He also was loved by the embassy staff, because he treated them well, even opening up the pool at Taverna for staff use, something no other ambassador had done.

He never lost the simple, personal touch that he learned growing up on the streets of South Philly.

Tommy always made us proud.

James Casto is retired from the Huntington, W. Va., Herald-Dispatch. This column appeared August 15, 2004.

Summertime Recollections
From Way Back When

The days are flying by. Summer 2004 is almost over. Labor Day, the unofficial end of summer, is just around the corner.

When I was a boy in Huntington back in the '50s, summer was one fun-filled day after another.

You could play cops and robbers, or cowboys and Indians (er, make that Native Americans), or be a brave space explorer landing on the moon. You could use a metal garbage can lid as an improvised shield, and an old curtain rod as a make-believe sword and pretend you were one of the knights at King Arthur's Round Table.

Or you could draw a big circle in the dirt and be a circus ringmaster. Or maybe that fearless animal tamer Frank Buck putting a cage of imaginary lions through their paces.

Speaking of circles, you could draw a ring and shoot marbles with the other fellows. I soon learned, however, that I was better off not playing "for keeps," as I was so hopelessly inept that it didn't take long before I was cleaned out, with nary a marble to my name.

You could collect bottle caps and see how many different ones you could find.

When I somehow came into possession of a sales receipt book, I became an impromptu police officer, going around and writing down car license numbers – keeping a wary eye peeled for out-of-state tags, sure to belong to strangers in town for some nefarious purpose.

I often had chores to do – keeping the lawn cut, trimming the dinky little hedge in front of our house and other tasks.

But once these jobs were done and my mother had dug in her pocketbook for a quarter or two, it was off to the movies. You could go on Saturday afternoons all year long, of course. But in summers you could go any afternoon you liked – and more than once a week if you had enough quarters.

When I got a bit older, it was exciting to board one of those big clunkers operated by the Ohio Valley Bus Co. and venture off to Dreamland Pool for the day. Or maybe go exploring in the "wilds" of Ritter Park.

Then there were summertime picnics with fried chicken and deviled eggs and corn on the cob ("Wipe your chin, Jimmy") and big dill pickles and watermelon and – surely best of all – home-made ice cream from a hand-cranked freezer.

I remember lying on my back in the summer grass and watching the white clouds work their way across the sky. Sometimes they moved so slowly you could barely see it. Other times, they skidded along as if in their own curious race.

For some reason, I've always loved thunderstorms. And is there a better place to watch a summer storm than your own front porch, where you're snug and dry?

That old porch swing was also a perfect place for summertime reading.

That's what summer was like if you were young in Huntington in the 1950s, before parents decided that summertime fun for their youngsters had to be organized. And before computers and video games came along to monopolize young minds and imaginations.

April 18, 2004

The Sad (And High) Cost Of Progress

Vinson C. Bell died this week, and with his passing we lost another link to the day when many of Huntington's neighborhoods were home to small, family-owned businesses.

"Mr. Bell" – I would never dream of referring to him otherwise – died Tuesday. He was 95.

For more than 30 years, he and his late wife, Myrtle, operated Bell's Food Market on the northeast corner of 3rd Avenue and what was then 16th Street (now Hal Greer Boulevard).

I grew up only two blocks or so from there, and if I had a dollar for every time my mother dispatched me to Bell's Market on a last-minute mission, I wouldn't have to worry about the ups and downs of my 401K.

Mother loved to bake and although she was by no means scatterbrained, it often seemed that when it came time to add a crucial item, there would be none at hand. So I would hear her call: "Jimmy, come quick. I need you to run to the store for me."

And off I went to fetch the needed butter or sugar or whatever. Out the back door I went, down the alley and around the corner to Bell's.

I seldom minded the interruption in whatever I was doing. Besides, I generally was told I could buy a 5-cent candy bar while I was there.

The tiny store building was crammed with foodstuffs, and it was always fun to watch Mr. Bell use a long pole to retrieve items – a box of Wheaties, say – from one of the top shelves. It was even more fun when, as sometimes happened, the falling box landed on his head.

I remember, besides my own frequent missions to Bell's, the Saturday morning ritual when Mother would call the store and dictate her weekly shopping list to Mrs. Bell, who later would fill the order and have it carried to our back door.

But what I remember most about Bell's Market was when – more than once -- we had no money for that week's groceries and they were delivered to our door just the same.

"I know you'll pay me when you can," Mr. Bell assured my stepfather. And indeed that was the case.

Try that at Wal-Mart.

The Bells closed their grocery store many years ago, of course. It's long gone, consigned to memory.

Gone, too, is Marshall Sundries, the neighborhood drug store at 4th Avenue and 15th Street where I could buy a cherry Coke and read the comic books for free until Harry, the soda jerk, decided my time was up and pointed to the door.

Long gone as well is nearby Roberts' Esso, where a uniformed attendant actually pumped the gas for you, while cleaning the windshield and asking if you needed a free road map.

Neighborhood groceries, corner drug stores, mom-and-pop gas stations – they've all vanished, victims of what's called "progress."

But that progress, it seems to me, has come at a dear price.

Tom Purcell is a syndicated columnist. His books include "An Apple Core, a Toilet: Misadventures of a 1970s Childhood." This column appeared April 21, 2009.

I'm Turning Into My Dad,
But That's A Good Thing

My father was born in 1933. He was a paperboy in the days when paperboys stood on city corners and shouted, "Extra!"

In my father's home, the newspaper still is king. He has two delivered daily. He reads every inch of both. He does the crossword puzzle in both, too – with a pencil.

(Note to people under 25: A pencil is a small, yellow stick that leaves a mark when its tip is pressed against paper.)

My father knows that people can do crossword puzzles on their computers – and cell phones and BlackBerrys – but the idea is nutty to him. Only an idiot would bring electronic equipment into the bathroom.

To be sure, my father has shunned the communications marvels of modern times. He uses my mother's cell phone – but only to avoid long-distance charges.

He has never sent or received email.

He never searches the web. He uses the White Pages or Yellow Pages.

(Note to people under 35: The White and Yellow Pages are thick directories of people and businesses that are left at your door once a year.)

And there are two other things my father will never do: use Facebook or Twitter.

Facebook.com is a social-networking web site where people post important updates for their electronic "friends," such as detailed descriptions of what they had for breakfast.

Twitter.com is similar to Facebook, except the descriptions are brief (140 characters or less): "Ate oatmeal today. Was good."

There certainly are upsides to these technologies.

The Wall Street Journal reports that Twitter – with its ability to rapid-fire messages to millions – can be a powerful communications tool. Sure, celebrities use it to update fans on their latest banalities, but emergency organizations are also using it to alert people during disasters.

As for Facebook, it is surely helpful to stay-at-home parents who are isolated from other adults. There is an upside to swapping personal information, even if it is over the Internet.

Facebook has helped me locate – and be located by – friends I haven't talked to for years. Some 300 million are using the tool; there is a good chance people from your past are using the site, too.

Which brings us to the downside.

Maybe there is a reason your old friends and old girlfriends are old friends and old girlfriends. Maybe

you've already told them everything you had to say –
with the exception of what you just ate for breakfast.

I was at a party recently where I was accused of
being "old" – I'm 46 – because I have never "drunk-
texted" friends (or old friends or girlfriends).

(Note to people over 50: Texting is when you press
both thumbs against a miniature cell phone keypad to
bastardize the English language).

My generation preferred to "drunk-email" old friends
and girlfriends. The generation before mine preferred
to "drunk-phone call." My father's generation would
"drunk walk to the person's house and knock on the
door."

In any event, recent reports suggest that people are
tiring of technology-enabled social networking.

Craig Kinsley, a professor of neuroscience at the
University of Richmond, told the Associated Press
why: Humans crave contact and human interaction, but
interaction over the Internet is without substance.

Which brings us to my father.

He hasn't wasted a moment on superficial online
communications. He is doing just great in the real
world of the White Pages, printed newspapers and
books.

(Note to people under 25: A book is a compact
device in which words are printed on several pieces of
paper; the paper is glued to a spine).

When my father wants to communicate, he
approaches other human beings --usually my mother --
and uses his voice. Sometimes he uses facial
expressions to emphasize a point.

I think he is on to something.

Although I'm beginning to use Twitter for useful and interesting updates – and LinkedIn.com for business networking – I don't use Facebook much any more. I prefer to meet people for breakfast (and see firsthand what they're eating).

As I said, I'm turning into my father. Thank goodness.

November 9, 2013

Let's Remember The Loved Ones Of Soldiers, Too

Ida Ayres never served a day in the Armed Forces, but she knows a thing or two about the sacrifices of war.

When we think of war and conflict, we think of the men and women who put themselves in harm's way, as we should. But what about the parents, children, siblings and spouses who are left behind to worry and pray?

"Through four wars, I have been the daughter, sister, wife and mother of men who served their country," Ida explained to me.

During World War I, Ida's father, Sam DiRenna, fought for the Italian army. DiRenna, who was born in a small town near Naples, was captured by the Germans and spent four years in a concentration camp. He survived by eating potato peels and garbage scraps. The Germans branded his forehead – a scar he retained for the rest of his life.

Thankfully, he lived. He was declared a hero in Italy for overcoming the brutality. He eventually settled in America. He sent for his wife. They gave birth to Ida and two sons, Angelo and Pasquale. Life was hard during the Depression, but Ida's family prevailed.

But then America was thrust back into war – a war in which both of Ida's brothers would serve. In 1944, Angelo enlisted in the Navy. Pasquale followed in 1945. Angelo was stationed on LST 1040 and Pasquale served on a carrier.

Their letters home arrived every three or four weeks. Then Angelo's stopped coming. Six months passed without a word. Ida was distraught, her mother barely able to function. Finally, word came that Angelo's ship had been in a typhoon. But he survived.

Both brothers returned home and the world was finally settling down. The economy grew at a rapid rate. Ida eventually married and bore two sons. Her husband Harry had fought in Korea before they met (he doctored his birth certificate and found himself on the front lines as a 16-year-old kid). After the wedding, he was called to serve another tour in Korea, Thankfully, he returned home safely.

But in 1966, her husband was called back again. This time he left his wife and two sons behind to fight in Vietnam. As an Army major, he was lucky to survive 12 months of dangerous air missions. In one battle, his best friend had both arms and legs shot off right next to him.

In 1968, Ida's oldest son Sam announced he was eager to join his father in Vietnam. Fresh out of high school at 17, Sam enlisted and became a medic. The young man saw some of the worst horrors that war produced, horrors that are with him still.

Thankfully, both Harry and Sam made it home. Finally, Ida hoped, life could get back to normal. And for the most part, life did. America went on to enjoy an amazing run of prosperity. We were riding high until 9/11, when we were thrust into another conflict.

And now Ida's youngest son, Major General Tim Ayres – my childhood friend – has completed several deployments in Afghanistan and Iraq. The U.S. Army recently awarded him his second star and appointed him Deputy Judge Advocate General.

According to the Department of Veterans Affairs, Memorial Day is about remembering and honoring soldiers who died serving their country. Veterans Day, however, is about thanking and honoring all members of the military, whether they served during times or war or times of peace.

This Veterans Day, as we thank and honor those who have served, we should also pay homage to people like Ida Ayres – the parents, children, siblings and spouses who have quietly sacrificed for their country.

Dorothy Rosby is a syndicated humor columnist whose work has appeared in 11 Western and Midwestern states since 1996. She lives in Rapid City, S.D. This column ran in 2013.

Changing The Game In Romance

My, how things change! Early in our courtship, my husband took me to Game Six of the 1987 World Series. Twenty-some years later, he drove me to a colonoscopy.

Early in our marriage, we went on a hot air balloon ride. A few months ago, we went to see a tax preparer. That's how it is. Before marriage, you paint the town. After marriage, you paint the house.

As the wedding season gets under way, I think it's important that couples be made aware of this phenomenon, lest they become disheartened the first time their honey bunch does something that shows he or she is a mere mortal after all.

But first let me say, there's nothing quite as hard on a marriage as publishing details about your own. So I'm going to focus on changes that happen in most marriages. Whether or not they've happened in mine, I'm not saying, and my husband had better not either.

Brides and grooms-to-be, what follows is my wedding gift to you. I realize it wasn't on your registry.

Ladies, right now you're attracted to your man because of his charm, personality and good looks. You won't believe this, but after you're married, you'll find him most attractive when he's doing dishes. In fact, there's only one time you'll find him more attractive, and that's when he's changing a diaper.

Men, early in your marriage, your wife will greet you with a kiss when you come home. After a few years, she'll just call up from the basement, "Did you remember to pick up milk?"

Brides, now you dress up before you see your man. After a few years, you'll dress up for lunch with your girlfriends and wear your favorite sweatpants when you're with him. But it's OK, men; you won't notice what she's wearing anyway.

Right now, neither of you can imagine why any couple would want a king-sized bed. But the day will come when no bed is big enough. What you'll want is a duplex. It's not that you won't want to cuddle any more. It's that one of you will have become a snorer. If you're lucky, the other one will have become hard of hearing.

By the way, when you're asked to promise, "For better or worse," at your wedding, snoring is what they mean by "worse."

I know I've painted a bleak picture, but don't be discouraged. Some of these changes will happen simply because you'll get old. I'm joking. Sort of.

Mainly, your relationship will change because you'll give up trying to make a good impression. Ladies, there's no sense in trying to impress someone who's watched you give birth.

Men, you won't be able to impress her any more either, not after she's seen you with the stomach flu, or coming up the driveway on a brand new motorcycle you didn't discuss with her.

Together you'll have a family, borrow money, and spend more time with the in-laws than you'd like. It's hard to have illusions after events like these. But eventually you'll make the transition from "in love" to "unconditional love," a more enduring, if less interesting condition.

After all, marriage is about partnering up on the business of daily life, and much of that is less than romantic. And a wedding is like the 1987 World Series. The Twins won. They had a big party. Then a few months later, they were at spring training.

This Rosby piece appeared in 2012.

What Hath Bell Wrought?

The first words ever spoken on a telephone were those of inventor Alexander Graham Bell to his assistant, Thomas Watson, on March 10, 1876: "Mr. Watson, come here. I want to see you." These words not only marked the beginning of telephone history, they are also the first documented example of poor telephone manners.

No "hello." No "please." No, "Am I getting you at a bad time?"

I suppose we can forgive Bell for his lack of courtesy. He must have been terribly excited, what with inventing the gizmo that would revolutionize communication and make it possible to win radio call-in contests. And Watson may not have taken offense anyway; he was probably thrilled he wouldn't have to order his pizza by mail any more.

But these days, we need to be more cognizant of telephone etiquette. While telephones have evolved to the point they can do everything but shine your shoes, telephone manners started out badly and went down line from there.

I don't mean to imply that I am above poor telephone manners myself. I'm not old enough to have used a party line, but if I'd grown up with one, I can assure you I would have listened in on my neighbors. Had Bell's telephone been on a party line, his first words might have been, "Mr. Watson, come here. I don't want Mr. Johnson and Mrs. Smith to hear what I have to say."

At some point, party lines went away and the only people who could listen in on telephone calls were family members. (I know this, because I did it.) There were telephones in every home and they were ringing at all hours of the day and night. Watson might have answered that first historic call with, "Mr. Bell, I told you not to call me during dinner."

Eventually, phone booths popped up everywhere, paving the way for Superman comics and creating a whole new set of issues. If he'd built one of those right away, Bell would have had to borrow a quarter to make that first call.

And then along came the answering machine: "Mr. Watson, pick up the phone. I know you're there."

Then there was the cordless phone, which my family lovingly refers to as the "walk-around phone" when we can find it and the "walk-away phone" when we can't. Had Bell invented it right away, he would have had to ask his assistant for help before making his first call. "Mr. Watson, where's the telephone?" "The what, sir?"

We're all lucky Bell didn't start out with call-waiting. Who knows how things would be different if Watson had answered that first momentous call with, "Let me put you on hold. I've got another call. Joking!"

Or what if Bell's first telephone had caller ID, allowing Watson to screen his calls. "I'm not answering that. Mr. Bell is bossy and has no manners!"

Then there was the cell phone and a return to eavesdropping – except cell phones aren't as efficient as party lines because we can only hear one side of the conversation. Fortunately, Bell could have kept his message private by texting, "Mr. Watson, come here." And Mr. Watson would have texted back, "No need to text me, sir. I'm in the same room."

Had Bell's first phone been a Smartphone, Watson would have been too busy playing Candy Crush or changing his ring tones to answer the call. Bell would have stomped down the hall, taken a look at his once loyal assistant, and said, "Oh, Mr. Watson! What have I done?"

And Watson would have replied, "Quick, Mr. Bell! Let's take a selfie!"

Arthur Henry Gunther III wrote columns for the Journal-News in Nyack, N.Y., from 1964 until 2006. This piece ran August 16, 2010.

Adventure Inside The Old 5&10

You can be as old as I am – 67 – and still be age 12 when you step into the 2010 version of a 5&10-cent store. You can have $200 in your pocket, but again feel the wonder of what a quarter might buy in this magical place.

Once, every downtown had a 5&10, sometimes two. Usually there was the omnipresent Woolworth's, where in my grandparents' time many items did indeed sell for a nickel or a dime. In the 1950s, in Spring Valley, N.Y., at the Consolidated 5&10, 25 cents and up was more likely.

Nyack, a nearby village, had two dime stores and each was set up in honorable, cherished fashion. Double-entry doors to the right, double exit to the left. Railroad flat floor plan, a shotgun drive in a long room. Wooden floors once varnished, but never again. Islands of counters with five-inch glass walls, goods spread neatly.

(An odd thing about those counters. They never seemed messy, even on a sale day when dish towels, for example, might be on special at 10 cents per. Maybe consumers were neater then. Today, in major department stores, counters without glass walls but with originally well-stacked piles of say, shirts, soon become jungles of goods in disarray.)

In the old 5&10, hardware items were usually toward the back of the store, and that's where I headed. Once, with 25 cents in hand, I could not wait until Boy Scout Troop 13 had finished its Friday night meeting at the Dutch Reformed Church so I could get over to Consolidated, zoom down the long aisle to the right, back to the last glass-walled counter and then to the small bottles of turpentine. I got one for 19 cents, no tax, and once out of the store and on my walk home to Hillcrest, I opened it to get the pine smell. The next day, it was used on a wood-working project in my parents' unfinished basement.

In larger downtowns, the dime stores had candy counters where you bought by the pound or fraction thereof. Loose candy – nonpareils were a favorite – were scooped up by the counter person, weighed in a hopper and then slid into a white paper bag, which you clutched tightly all the way home.

Other 5&10s had wonderful donut counters, and as soon as you entered the store you could smell the sweetness. Every mom's hand was soon tugged by a child with a watering mouth. Even bigger stores had lunch counters with fountain service and quick, simple sandwiches, such as grilled cheese and chicken salad.

Just as Automats were once urban fixtures, complete with characters and good, dependable food, so 5&10s were small and big downtown meccas, one of the required stores that made main street Main Street -- a place for every income level, almost always affordable, even for a fellow with a rare quarter burning a hole in his pocket.

What an adventure they were.

Have Yourself A Simple Good
Time At The Post Office

In a very simple time when things were still complicated for grown-ups, of course, country children of the 1940s and '50s found diversion in rustling through the woods, playing hide-and-seek with other kids and going on small errands with dad or mom.

Absent the video games, cell phones, Twitter, Facebook, HDTV, ballet school, karate lessons and all the other appointments now penciled in the datebook of a youngster – if you were staring at the wall as a 7-year-old and your dad was warming up the 1949 Studebaker Commander – he might beckon you to hop in and travel the few miles to the Spring Valley, N.Y., Post Office so he could receive mail from Box 74.

You weren't tall enough to see in the small box, set in a long row of decorative brass containers with combination locks. In a year or two, you could actually open the box yourself, anticipating mail as you walked home from school.

But, for now, Dad went to get what was there, and you would hang around the Art Deco lobby, standing on a grand marble floor and looking up at the Social Realism mural, courtesy of the Franklin D. Roosevelt and Postmaster Jim Farley Post Office rebuilding projects of the Depression.

The Spring Valley branch on Madison Avenue was and is a most solid structure, meant to convey the ability of a nation to rebuild itself and to endure. And the inside was deliberately set as a small palace, with wonderful hissing steam that warmed you on the coldest of February days.

The government could help take care of you, you see, and the mural of laborers, farmers and industrial smokestacks billowing the white smoke of progress underscored this "We can do it" recovery.

A socialism-tainted view, though, was lost on the 7-year-old in 1949. He was there, escaping boredom with his father, and he liked getting his fingers warm at the radiator. He also wanted his own mail, so the routine was to head over to the huge wire basket where people threw junk mail that arrived even in those days, and without messing about too much, take out a sealed letter and hold it, then open it, a grown-up thing to do.

The trip home was usually uneventful. Dad might stop for a loaf of Sunshine Bread at Roth's Store, the motor and heater left running as he ran in and out. Soon you would be back in the quiet of the house, no TV to watch, and you might seek imagination in adjacent woods, within earshot of Mom calling you home for supper at about 5:15.

Like I said, a simple time.

Jim Spencer is currently the Washington correspondent for the Minneapolis Star-Tribune. Before that assignment, he wrote columns for the Denver Post and the Newport News, Va., Daily Press. This piece appeared in the Daily Press on January 15, 1997.

Holiday Card Is Reminder Of Blessings

The card depicts the ideal Christmas scene: a poinsettia garnished with sprays of holly spills from a giant vase on the front porch of a white clapboard house. A huge wreath hangs from the front door, which swings open to reveal an evergreen decorated with colorful ornaments and a floor full of brightly wrapped gift boxes. The printed message offers "Every Good Wish For Your Happiness This Holiday Season."

Pauline Trent taped two hopelessly wrinkled dollar bills to the inside cover of the card. Beneath them, in a shaky hand with a black ball-point pen, she wrote, "God bless you and your family. P.S. Thank you for being so wonderful."

I have carried this card year-'round in my briefcase since receiving it in January of 1994. I intend to carry it until I retire. Then it will become an heirloom that I hope my grandchildren's grandchildren will hold dear.

Sometimes, when I give a speech, I pull out Ms. Trent's card, show it to the audience and tell the story about how I got it. Otherwise, it simply stays with me, not as a good luck charm, but as a reminder that what you see depends on where you look.

I'm not sure Pauline Trent ever saw a Christmas like the one on the card she gave me. In the last five years I know she certainly didn't. Ms. Trent lived in a run-down brick bungalow on 24th Street in Newport News. There wasn't a white clapboard in sight. No flourishing poinsettias graced her porch in the time that I delivered Meals on Wheels to her. No wreaths hung from her door. No freshly cut pine covered in ornaments livened up her living room.

In fact, at the time I received her Christmas card I had visited Ms. Trent almost every week for several years, but had never seen her. She was bedridden, I had been told, and didn't care to have anyone see her that way.

So we became voices who passed in the day. Most Wednesdays, I drove to her bleak, crime-infested neighborhood, opened her unlocked door, announced my presence loudly so she wouldn't be alarmed and left her meal on the end table in the living room.

"God bless you," she called out from the back of the house as I left.

"And God bless you," I called back as I let myself out and locked her door against the mayhem of the street beyond.

That was it until three years ago, when, as I have done every Christmas season since I began delivering Meals on Wheels, I bought fresh fruit and cards to give to each of the clients on my route. I never expected anybody to give anything back. Least of all Ms. Trent.

But there was an envelope with my name on it waiting for me on the end table my first week back after the holiday and, inside it, the card and the money.

I can't foresee a circumstance in which I would part with either, especially since I read Ms. Trent's obituary in the paper last week.

I stopped delivering meals to her more than a year ago because she had gotten full-time home nursing care. Now I'm proud to say that before I stopped I finally did get to see Pauline Trent. We met face-to-face because she moved to a specially equipped bed too big to fit anywhere in her house except the living room. The new bed became necessary after she fell, knocked herself out and spent several weeks in the hospital.

"The nurses called me Heaven because I thought I had died," she told me. "When I woke up in the hospital, I asked, 'Is this heaven?'"

No, heaven is a place in the spirit where illness and poverty cannot penetrate. I have a picture of it right here in my briefcase if you want to take a look.

This Spencer column ran July 12, 2004, in the Denver Post.

Longtime Shop Owners Maintain Old-Fashioned Work Ethic

AURORA, Colo. – The trucks, 1946 Studebaker and a 1952 International, rest in peace behind the workshop at Comet Gas Co. Inc. They ended up there after years of faithful service hauling propane to Tom and Bertha Earnest's customers.

And that's where they'll stay.

"I figured they did their work," Tom Earnest said. "I didn't want to junk 'em."

Earnest, 71, has a unique relationship with the machines and equipment that surround him at the family business he and his wife started July 1, 1964, near the corner of Colfax Avenue and Tower Road. He says he can feel their "aches and pains."

"When it comes to throwing something away, I just don't," he explained. "I came through the damn Depression. You don't forget."

So he doctors everything he can in a workshop that is a mechanic's paradise. He built it with a high ceiling to keep it cool, then stuffed it with enough equipment to keep an army running which, incidentally, is what Earnest did roughly 50 years ago.

"I got the biggest amount of my education in Germany in the Army engineers," he said. "All we had was junk left over after World War II. We couldn't get parts. We had to make 'em."

He still fabricates anything having to do with compressed gas in a workshop cluttered with the abandon of an artist's studio. Hoses and giant wrenches hang from the walls. Huge vises, jacks and generators dot the floor, sharing room with a 1926 Model T Ford and a 1954 Hudson Hornet. Bench grinders compete for space with welding gear and a drill press dusted with gleaming metal shavings. Valves and fittings lie everywhere.

Comet Gas sells propane as its primary calling. Thousands of tanks, ranging from backyard grill-size to a 60-foot-long, 8-foot-high behemoth that doubles as a

sign take up most of the company's space. But like a
dying generation of American small-business owners,
Tom and Bertha Earnest are about more than the so-
called service economy. They know how to do, not just
how to sell.

"I put all my own tanks on my trucks (for delivery),"
Tom said, pointing at a crane capable of lifting 14,500
pounds. "I don't farm anything out.

"If you're enjoying what you're doing, there's no work
to it."

It's more than a matter of business; it's a matter of
pride. On a recent day, Tom Earnest split his time
between filling tanks and installing a propane system that
would run a forge and welding equipment on a
blacksmith's truck. He also maintains recreational
vehicles and repairs compressed-gas equipment for the
Colorado Department of Transportation.

That's the way it's been, six days a week, for 40 years.
The Earnests get to work at 7 a.m. These days, they join
Wolfgang, the white German shepherd who guards the
property 24/7.

"Sometimes we worked until midnight delivering
propane when we first started," said Bertha, 74, the self-
described "head bookkeeper" of Comet Gas. "We're old
hat."

Old enough, said her husband, to "remember taking a
handshake for a year's business from a farmer and never
having to worry about getting paid."

Times change. His propane deals with farmers in
Western Kansas died years ago.

Some of today's customers aren't as trustworthy as the
salt of the Earth with whom the Earnests once dealt.

Vandals have chucked rocks through the windshields of some old vehicles on the back of the lot. A mailbox bolted atop an empty oxygen cylinder and planted in the ground by the driveway got beat up so often that Tom finally took it down.

But the mom and pop of this mom-and-pop business keep coming back. And so do the customers.

A prayer hanging on the wall at Comet Gas offers a clue why.

"Lord," says the wall hanging, "let me be just half the person my dog thinks I am."

Tom and Bertha Earnest are way beyond that.

Louise Leslie, retired editor and columnist for the Clinch Valley News in Tazewell, Va., wrote this piece in 1995. She has been writing columns for more than 50 years.

Rush Campbell And Wooden Shoes

Rush Campbell was the only real hobo I've known. When I was a child, he appeared in Tazewell each spring along with the robins and daffodils. He would come to our house and ask for work. For me, the magic season came with him.

As he worked, Rush Campbell told stories. He had been everywhere and loved to talk about his journeys. He had ridden elephants in India and camels in Egypt. He had climbed the highest mountains and sailed the roughest seas.

In his wanderings, Rush had been to the Arctic and the Amazon jungle. He had met kings and peasants and they were all his friends. One day, he told me he had been to Alcatraz, and I believed that, too.

Rush Campbell smiled while he hoed the garden and cut the grass. His eyes sparkled when he told his tales and fueled the imagination of a 10-year-old girl. I was determined to go everywhere he had been, even Alcatraz. At that time, I wanted to hop freight trains like Rush did and sail on ships and walk over dusty trails. He knew what was beyond Clinch Mountain, and I wanted to follow him.

In late summer when there was a tingle in the air, he would be restless and absent-minded. He would stop his work and gaze into the distance when he heard the train

whistle from across the hill. I knew what to expect. The next day he was gone, without saying a word of farewell. I would wait for Rush each morning, but it would be another spring before he came to the door with new stories and dancing eyes.

One sunny day, after I had learned all the third-grade books, Rush talked as I followed him in the garden. His wanderings that year had taken him to European capitals and the haunts of the Orient. He had lived for a while with an Indian tribe before sailing around the tip of South America.

He said, "I've been to Hawaii where everybody wears wooden shoes." With all my third-grade knowledge, I answered, "I thought they wore wooden shoes in Holland." Rush was silent, but he looked at me with a strange sadness in his eyes.

I remember a scared feeling in the pit of my stomach. I had punched a hole in his dream world, and in mine. I couldn't snatch it back. I didn't understand, but he realized I had crossed the magic line into the world of doubts.

The next spring, the robins came and the daffodils bloomed, but Rush did not come back. I never saw him again, and now I can't find anybody who remembers him. Maybe he decided to live on that Pacific island he told me about. He was a tribal chief in Borneo, he said, so perhaps he stayed in that kingdom.

Maybe he went to Holland to see the wooden shoes. Sometimes I wonder if he couldn't face a little girl who didn't believe any more.

Leslie penned this column in 1990.

A Lock Of Long-Kept Hair

I remember my grandfather Rhudy as an old man with a long, white beard and dancing eyes. Because I recall his laughter and his kindness, I can tell his story. It's the story of a young Levi Rhudy growing up in Burkes Garden (in Tazewell County), a romantic young man who let his granddaughter discovery a mystery, never to be solved.

It started, unromantically, a few months ago when I was cleaning my basement. I dusted a small, black suitcase that sat on a high shelf. I've seen the suitcase many times before and I've always known it belonged to my grandfather. But this was the first time I carefully studied the contents.

Along with old newspaper clippings and outdated schoolbooks, I found a small pouch tucked in a side pocket. Inside was a long lock of blond hair. It was fresh, silky and shiny, and appeared to have never been moved from its hiding place. It was a small part of my grandfather's life that had been hidden for well over a century.

Whose lock of hair did he treasure for a lifetime? What memory stayed with him through the years of tending a Burkes Garden farm and raising a family? When I held the lock of hair I had a glimpse, it seemed, of a man so different from the quiet, reserved grandfather I remember in his last years. What story did he hold inside, never telling?

The romantic custom of saving locks of hair is out of style now. It belongs to the world of Dickens and Jane Austen, and perhaps to the farms in Burkes Garden in the mid-19th century. I savor this tangible evidence of a young man who dreamed dreams a granddaughter can understand.

Without knowing my grandfather's story, I have followed in his footsteps. Hidden away in a diary I have a lock of hair that belonged to a sea captain I once knew. When I look at it, I touch foreign soil and remember times seldom mentioned, and I feel the wind beneath my wings.

Donna Clements writes a self-syndicated opinion column. She has her own publishing company, World Pearls Press. This column appeared in the Roanoke Rapids, N.C., Daily Herald on October 16, 2013.

Of Tobacco And "Talking" Feet

Autumn causes me to revisit my memories of growing up on a tobacco farm more than any other season of the year.

More than early springtime when seeds are sown in a plant bed and then covered with a big white sheet providing nurturing shelter for strong, healthy plant development, and more than the early summer, when those plants are transplanted into fields of uniform rows. Even more than the late summer, which you would think would provide the most prolific memories because that is when the bulk of the work is done.

But it is fall that carved the shape of a tobacco leaf into my soul.

During the fall, the last of the "pullings" would take place, meaning what leaves were remaining on the stalk were harvested and placed in the barns for curing. People ask when they see a field of tobacco, why does it look like the leaves have been stripped from the plant, bottom-sides upward? The answer is, because they were.

The sun ripens the lower leaves first, so they are harvested first. The top leaves ripen last, so they are harvested last. So the next time you pass by a tobacco farm and see Q-tip-looking stalks standing erect in the fields, with a few leaves still glued to their tops, you will understand how that came to be and that they are in the final stage of being harvested.

The months of September and October were busy with the last of the duties required in wrapping up another growing season. School would have started for me, so the work that had to be done would take place before the first bell rang in the morning, or after the last bell in the afternoon. The chore of "taking down a barn of tobacco" was the most involved.

I would get up early with my daddy and maybe one other helper, and we would drive to the barn with the mist of the morning still hanging on for dear life. Everything was cold (or cool) and wet (or moist). We would arrange the poles in the barn until they were all layered like a six-layer yellow cake with milk chocolate icing on the back of the truck or the trailer.

One of the kindest old gentlemen who helped us through the years was named Solomon. He was a funny man and wore shoes with the toes cut out because he said his feet were always "talking." Everyone agreed with him, and we would fight over who had to stand beneath him in the barn with our noses at sniffing level of his "talking" feet. But he was the bravest of men, too, for he had no fear of the heights required to climb to the very top of the barn. Like his Old Testament namesake, he was wise and we always trusted him to be attentive, alert and aware of his surroundings and to whom he was passing. The sticks of cured tobacco weighed much less coming down than the green tobacco did being passed to the top, but it was still a precarious, awkward setting to handle it all without harm coming to anyone.

In addition to Solomon's "talking" shoes, the smell of the cured tobacco was intense because of the aroma of the fuel used during its drying time. A smell I would describe as the smell in the parking lot of a truck stop next to a tobacco shop, but even that does not come close.

I remember on the mornings when I didn't have time to return home to shower, I would go to school with bits of tobacco floating in my hair. I remember a particular morning when I was running late and had to go to the principal's office for a pass. As I was signing the excuse form, a piece of tobacco floated down to the paper. But it wasn't embarrassing. It represented hard work and determination. It represented everything my family stood for and everything we worked so hard to attain.

It represented fall and harvest and crisp mornings and the smell of Solomon's feet before breakfast.

April 7, 2011

Filling The Senses With Boxwoods

One of my childhood's strongest mental impressions is the field trip I took with my fourth-grade class to Colonial Williamsburg in Virginia. My senses were stimulated and indelibly engraved by the great calligraphy pen called memory.

My sense of sight viewed in vivid VistaVision the motion picture, "Williamsburg: The Story of a Patriot." My sense of touch felt the roughness of the handmade,

Virginian clay bricks, the embodiment of colonial architecture. Audibly, I recall the reverberating bass tones made by the cannons when fired, and my sense of taste --well, there's not much to be said about the PB&J on Wonder Bread in my brown bag lunch. Scent is scientifically considered to be the venerable key to unlocking our oldest and most vibrant memories, a fact proven by the earthy rich scent of boxwoods, which grabbed my heart and from that day to this and has never released its grip.

Used to structure gardens, these stately evergreen shrubs (some of them celebrating 150 years of existence) remain as evidence to the everlastingness of the New World.

So when I came to know Pete and Kathryn Floyd, of Kathryn's Shrubs in Northampton County, and became engulfed in the clutches of the thousands of boxwoods they nurture with parental pride, I slipped back in time — back to one of my dearest memories.

As you travel along Highway 305 from Jackson towards Rich Square, the peaceful temperaments emanating from the potted boxwoods (and the Floyds) magnetically pull you into their fold. You see the deep hues of green; you touch the velvety textures of green; you hear and smell the tranquil nothingness of green.

The hovering mama and papa visibly wear their joy. It is as evident as the flecks of sunshine filtering through the tops of the pines toward the orderly, synchronized plants like toy soldiers -- perfectly aligned because the large number of plants and the lengthy growing process demand it. There are English, American, and Japanese boxwoods — the common varieties as well as several hybrids that naturally form perfect spheres or angular pyramids, rare hybrids that have been developed by Mr. Floyd.

If a plant is bought, Mr. Floyd seeks a silent commitment of care with his eyes. It is very binding. Yes, aromas open the chambers of the heart as a child's recognition of his mother through a scant scent of lavender soap; a pair of lovers' identification with the concentrated oil of a rose; or a foraging stranger seeking familial aromas of home.

By meeting the Floyds and visiting their beautiful nursery and taking in the powerful scent of boxwoods experienced in my youth, I found my key.

Tom Rademacher writes for the Grand Rapids, Mich., Press. His books include "The Gift of CAKE," about disabled persons. This column appeared December 25, 2009.

Not Your Usual Teenager Volunteers At Nursing Home

GRANDVILLE, Mich. -- Even the best of them, on their best days, can't help but let a bit of pathos creep in the door. It's the bane of every nursing home—a place that might be teeming with kind employees and good food and a nature trail— but still is a last whistle stop for most, shades of gray all melding to black.

And then in walks a kid named Parker Ceplina, 6 feet of gangly and braces and all of 15.

Here's his sunny countenance day after day, volunteering his teenage clock at Brookcrest Nursing Home, choosing to be among men and women five and more decades his senior, and with what in common?

"It's just so rewarding," he says. "I just love it. It's just so much fun."

What is? Jigsaw puzzles? Cutting other people's food?

And he says yes. Exactly. "Because that's what gives them pleasure. And I'm fortunate enough to be in the right place at the right time to provide."

Fifteen. Do you remember? It was all about first dances and hanging out and going to parties and communing with classmates and the beginning stages of moon-howling.

But Parker Ceplina wants to arrange someone's afghan. Attend to a drooling lip. Play euchre if that's what they want. And when he grows up, perhaps work in recreational therapy at a place like Brookcrest.

"I can't pay him because he's not even 16 yet," says his boss, Christina Matzke, her voice almost in pain. And she pulls Parker's chart to demonstrate that during 2008, he volunteered 388 hours at Brookcrest.

By the time this year pulls to a close, Parker will have put in well over 600 hours, and that includes 73 in August alone—a month for soaking up the sun, playing tennis, owning the beach.

His role here originated with an eighth-grade project two years ago, in which students were expected to volunteer. He figured he'd go next door; that's how close he lives to Brookcrest.

Was it difficult at first?

"It was. Seeing them in pain."

Still, he couldn't help but fall in love with the place— both the residents and those who work there for pay. And so he attends classes at Lighthouse Academy in Kentwood, manages the school's basketball team, thrills to science classes, and spends his spare hours at Brookcrest.

He's not demonstrative. He just gives folks his attention, a rarity in today's Me World.

Follow him through the hallways, and it's "Hi Bob," "Hi Ralph," "Hi Martha."

He pulls up alongside Phyllis Talsma's right shoulder as she lies recumbent to ease the effects of cerebral palsy that has encapsulated her body since birth. He touches fingers that will never uncurl.

"Hi Phyllis."

She answers in a language all her own. Hi Parker.

Maybe that's the crux of it—that Parker Ceplina
speaks a language others his age might only master much
later in their lives, a potent mixture of empathy coupled
with a mature understanding that translates into, "I may
be here some day myself. "

Brookcrest's employees pray that when he gets a
driver's license next year, he won't bug out.

"I won't," Parker says.

He's earned the respect of everyone on staff. "I think
there are special people in this world who are meant to
do this," says Patricia Boult, a Brookcrest employee
going on 10 years. "Parker's just got that special thing
about him. He'll do anything we ask him to do."

Adds co-worker Martha Torreson: "I've never met a
kid quite like him. Everyone loves him."

Melbourne Krul is 73 and arrived here in April. For
"the long haul," he says. Like many other residents, he's
created a special bond with Parker. "If everybody was
like Parker," says Krul, "we'd have a better world."

His wife, Donna, 71, echoes the sentiment, marveling
at how Parker will accompany residents on the bus to
visit a Cracker Barrel Old Country Store, escort carolers
down the hall, help someone with a wheelchair, just sit
and talk.

Maybe Parker Ceplina is as much about Christmas as a
Savior who came to redeem the world. It's just that
Parker Ceplina is doing it by reaching out to one wobbly
hand at a time, making a difference with tin voices
pleading from atrophied bodies.

"He is," says Donna Krul, "a boy we all would want."

Two Families Grieve
As Tragedies Strike

In what precious time they squeezed out of this life together, Patrick Smith and his bride, Karen Kuzawa, taught us how to love. And maybe that's how we should remember them—not as a couple who had but 11 months as man and wife, but a rare twosome whose marriage ended tragically, yes, but also with a promise of hope for us all.

Karen Smith, 52, bade goodbye to her 50-year-old husband, Patrick, on Friday, at a funeral Mass where he was lifted up as the sort of person who met life on uncomplicated terms and made it all about others.

Less than a year earlier, Karen was living out an unlikely dream-come-true, piloting her wheelchair down the aisle to be united with her Patrick, the kid she had first come to know while both were attending special classes at Ottawa Hills High School in Grand Rapids.

He battled muscular dystrophy, while cerebral palsy rendered her unable to walk even one day of her life. But last August was a day in the sun to forget how different they were and join together as newlyweds.

Their storybook romance took a turn Monday that nobody saw coming, when the car Patrick was driving was struck broadside by another on the city's Northeast Side. He died hours later.

Those who attended Patrick's funeral at Blessed Sacrament Catholic Church were many of the same who'd blessed their nuptials. And almost to a person, they wondered not only "Why him?" but "Why them?"

"Even as a little kid, she always wanted to talk about her wedding," recalled first cousin Mary Kuzawa-Boman.

"It was all she ever talked about, to be like everyone else. And then that dream came true. Why would this happen to two people who would never hurt another soul?"

I first met Patrick and Karen last summer, and a column pronouncing their love and intended vows graced the front page of The Press on June 16. It had a special effect on readers, stirring them to stop and wonder what sort of things we've all taken for granted in our relationships.

Here were two people so in love that it was enough to simply share one another's time.

Their most outlandish date meant a meal in a mall food court or watching "Little House on the Prairie" together.

In recent weeks, Karen had convinced Patrick to recite the rosary with her in the evening. But on Thursday just prior to Mass, she prayed over his body alone, light streaming into the church foyer from a medley of skylights, sharing a last moment with the man who had provided her joy and companionship.

She inched her electric wheelchair close to his blue-gray casket and reached out with a crooked left arm to finger the same suit he had worn to their wedding.

"I'm telling him that I love him," she whispered, "and that will never go away.

"And that I thank God that we had the time we did.

"I've been crying myself to sleep, but I know that Patrick is sending me messages from the gates of heaven."

And then she wept.

Patrick worked 10 years at Wal-Mart on Alpine Avenue, and his open casket bore a certificate of appreciation from the retailer. It also held stuffed animals, testament to his love of all things warm, fuzzy, simple. He liked chocolate and Precious Moments and making sure Karen had what she needed, day and night.

The afternoon Patrick died, he'd spent the morning painting Karen's nails, something she wasn't able to do well herself. Later, he took some treats to her parents' home and was struck while returning to the North End apartment he shared with Karen.

Prosecutors are weighing whether to charge the other driver, who reportedly told police he ran a stop sign while gazing at flags in a cemetery.

"My heart goes out to him," said Patrick's grieving brother, Tim. "It could have been any of us."

During Mass, the Rev. George Darling reminded us that, while Patrick may have had an imperfect body, "he functioned with a perfect heart, a pure heart," one that celebrated others in the way we all deserve to be treated.

"God gives us burdens," the priest said, "and, sometimes, they don 't make sense, but all those burdens involve us loving another person.

"Today," he added, "we give Patrick back to God, who gave him to us."

Maybe the lesson for us all is that the final chapter in Patrick's life calls us to reassess how we treat others, how bound we are to each other, how there is someone out there for all of us.

By focusing on the story of a love gone too soon and the brittle tapestry that is our lives, maybe today a son will stop to pick a bouquet for his mother, a dad forego his paintbrush for a game of catch, other newlyweds appreciate what it is "to have and to hold."

Suzette Martinez Standring is a syndicated columnist and the author of "The Art of Column Writing." She is host and producer of a cable television show about the craft of writing. This piece appeared October 30, 2009.

Incest Victim Wants To Conquer The Guilt

The taboo against incest is so great, victims often feel buried alive, mummified in shame.

In Massachusetts, a report revised in 2009 by the Department of Children and Families gives the following statistics: 78 percent of sexually abused children are female, most numerous at the ages of 14-16 years. The number of male victims peaks at 5-6 years old and at age 14. Of all children sexually abused, 40 per cent are white, 22 percent Hispanic, and 9 percent black. Fathers are the most significant perpetrators of sexual abuse.

National silence was shattered when actress Mackenzie Phillips revealed an incestuous relationship with her father, John Phillips, the now deceased leader of the Mamas and Papas.

He corrupted her childhood by introducing her to drugs as a young girl. Many hailed her as a hero for speaking out, but some family members insisted they were lies. Others questioned the actress' story based on her past as a drug abuser.

At age 67, "Elizabeth" is also an incest survivor. The Quincy, Mass., woman won't divulge her real identity because her sisters still hide the truth of what happened to them.

"Just because someone is ready doesn't mean everyone is ready at the same time. They want to protect their own secrets," she said.

The retired businesswoman applauds Phillips' determination to heal.

"What she did was fantastic. She wrote about it, she got it out in the public. It was her way of saying, 'Do what you want with it. I'm done with it. I don't want it any more,' " said Elizabeth.

Her alcoholic father, the sole breadwinner, violated her and her three sisters during their teenage years. He threatened to leave the family if Elizabeth told any one.

"I thought I was protecting my siblings. If I told my mom, she'd kick him out. Then we don't have any food. Who's going to work? Who's going to bring the money home?" she asked.

At the age of 12, Elizabeth was frightened that no one would believe her and that a divorce might place her in her father's custody. During those years she and her sisters never talked about it.

"When my mother went out, I could hear my father walk across the hall and I'd think he was coming to my room. I was relieved when he'd go to my sister," she recalled with guilty sadness.

After suffering through six years of incest, Elizabeth finally resisted her father and left home for good. For years she buried her memories, but the effects lingered. She abandoned Catholicism and became an atheist. She avoided her family. Her many relationships with men were plagued with trust and intimacy issues.

"It affected everything, but at the time I didn't know why. I felt guilty that I allowed it. I felt guilty about my sisters. I got severe headaches. It's a deep stress that can wreak havoc on your health, something of that magnitude," said Elizabeth, a cancer survivor.

Mackenzie Phillips was criticized when she used the word "consensual" to describe her involvement from the age of 19 to 29. Others saw it as rape or brainwashing.

Elizabeth said, "It's never consensual. What it becomes is familiar. Don't forget it started at a young age. He's the parent and you obey."

In her 40s, a traumatic date rape brought all the horror back. Later, menopause and all its hormonal changes churned up the long-buried turmoil and Elizabeth desperately wanted resolution.

"I went to the library, " she said, where she read books written by psychologists and incest survivors.

"It brought me to the reality that I was not to blame, that I wasn't alone, that I wasn't the bad child who allowed her father to do what he wanted. It gave me the strength to come out of the closet to speak about it."

But when she confronted her family, her efforts were met with anger and denial. Shortly afterward, her father died of a heart attack.

"In reality, he was drinking himself to oblivion," she said, adding, "He found an easy way out."

She was blamed for his death and to this day, her sisters will not talk about their experiences. But Elizabeth insists that letting go of her secret shame was profoundly healing. The exhausting weight of self-blame was lifted. The responsibility for corruption, manipulation and the perversion of a child's need for love sits squarely with the offender. Saying so out loud was liberating.

"I am happier, stronger, freer."

She feels sorry for those unable to voice their truth. Writing about the unspeakable can bring relief.

"If you can't tell your friends or family, put it down on paper, but bring it out somehow. You have to release this from your own thoughts. You were not the one who was wrong, no matter how old you were," she said.

If a survivor shares her story, Elizabeth advises one to set aside judgment or anger, however well-intentioned.

"Just be a good listener. It's like when somebody passes away, you can just say, 'I'm sorry.' "

Losing one's innocence, trust and sense of normalcy is like a death, but millions like Elizabeth are reclaiming their lives.

So confession is good for the soul?

"Yes, especially when you don't own the sin," she said.

March 4, 2006

Sharing The Last Days With Humorist Art Buchwald

Renowned columnist Art Buchwald has refused dialysis, and it's only a matter of time, maybe a short time, before he dies. For a man awaiting The Reaper, he's in unusually fine fettle.

I spent two days by his side to find Buchwald doesn't see himself as courageous, nor does he feel shored up by supernatural spiritual strength. To fade away naturally is the decision he made when faced with the alternative of a lifetime on dialysis.

He said, "I had two decisions. Continue dialysis, and that's boring to do three times a week, and I don't know where that's going, or I can just enjoy life and see where it takes me."

I arrived at his Washington, D.C., hospice to present to him the 2006 Ernie Pyle Lifetime Achievement Award from the National Society of Newspaper Columnists, since his June appearance at our Boston conference isn't likely. We wanted to lift his spirits.

February 28, the day I arrived, would have marked the fourth week since he stopped dialysis. That can't be good. What condition would he be in?

The word "raucous" came to mind when I found Buchwald in a lively gabfest with his family, as well as with Eunice and Maria Shriver. They were laughing it up over old memories and private jokes that bubbled over like champagne. Art, in a striped golf shirt and blue sweatpants, recently had his right leg amputated below the knee, but he never exhibited discomfort.

When presenting his award, I didn't know what was more nerve-wracking, trying to remember my little speech or having Eunice and Maria Shriver staring at me not two feet away.

Four days earlier, NPR aired a poignant interview between host Diane Rehm and Buchwald regarding his decision to forego further medical intervention.

Buchwald's candor was stunning, as he shared his fears (none), regrets (none) and any spiritual expectations (he's not sure, but probably none). Buchwald's number is coming up, and he wants to meet his fate squarely, sans any extraordinary means of delay, thank you very much.

"I've received unbelievable mail from people who agreed with me," he said.

A fat folder contained emails, cards and letters of salute and support, many composed during tears, according to their senders. Strangers wrote with relief, as if Buchwald's decision to captain his own destiny gave them permission some day to do so, too.

The willingness to jump overboard and wave off any lifeboat seems quite courageous, but Buchwald was unimpressed with the idea of bravery.

"I hated dialysis because it had to do with sitting there for five hours. It had to do with time. Once I made up my mind, that was it," he told me.

"The end" is not taboo talk. In fact, Buchwald finds funny fodder in knock-knock-knocking on heaven's door.

A nurse came up, "Mr. Buchwald, Tom Brokaw is on the line."

Buchwald took the call, laughing, "Hey, I'm still here and I don't know why…"

Once, when no celebrities were present to compete with, I pulled up a chair and asked him questions, like, "Art, why aren't you afraid of death?"

"Because I don't know what it is and I don't have control over it," he said.

"If you met God, what would he say to you?"

"There may or may not be a God, but I'm not going to be the one who is going to give the answers. Every religion is telling us there's one God, but I'm not sure, so I'm not giving it a lot of thought," he said.

His daughter asked, "Dad, did you ever have a near-death experience?"

Eighty-year-old Buchwald said, "Maybe during the war. It felt like near death in a foxhole when it was being mobbed. It wasn't a very pleasant thing."

"Here, at hospice, what thoughts bring you joy?" I asked.

"My children, the fact that it all came out pretty damn good. Making people laugh, getting joy out of that," he said.

Buchwald easily wrote about 8,000 columns during his 55-year career, according to Cathy Crary, his longtime assistant. He crafted three columns a week until about 1995, and penned two weekly until this past January.

I asked, "Art, do you miss writing? I know you're not doing your columns anymore, but are there moments when you're here and you wish you could just tap out one more column?"

"No, not really. I wrote a column, a sad one to run the day after I go to heaven," he said.

Through the windows, afternoon slices of sun gave the room a warm, lazy feel. This hospice was his last stop. Was it an uncomfortable thought?

Buchwald remained upbeat, "You gotta be somewhere and this is a pretty good place."

Then he took a nap.

Later Buchwald took a call from his business agent. Afterwards, I asked him, "Did you have a nice conversation?"

He said, "Yeah, I told him I'm amazed. There's no change."

I said, "Why are you amazed?"

"Because they said I'd be dead without dialysis. I'm not supposed to be doing this good," Buchwald said.

I said, "Maybe it's the power of positive thinking. Maybe you're being carried along on love."

Later, it was time to fly back to Boston, and Buchwald took my hand, "Thanks, honey, thanks for bringing the award."

"Art, any pearls of wisdom for all the columnists who love you?"

"Keep writing. Tell them to just keep writing," he said.